The Death of the English Pub

Christopher Hutt

Photographs by Iain Macmillan

Arrow Books

Arrow Books Ltd
3 Fitzroy Square, London W1

An Imprint of the Hutchinson Group

London Melbourne Sydney Auckland
Wellington Johannesburg Cape Town
and agencies throughout the world

First published by Arrow Books 1973

Filmset in Monophoto Apollo by
BAS Printers Limited, Wallop, Hampshire
Printed in Great Britain by Ebenezer Baylis & Son,
The Trinity Press, Worcester and bound by
G. & J. Kit-Kat Ltd, Shand Street, London SE1

ISBN 0 09 908020 6

Contents

Introduction

'When you have lost your Inns, drown your empty selves, for you will have lost the last of England.'

HILAIRE BELLOC

There is a pub in north-west London, which I sometimes visited during the early stages of research for this book. The public bar was a favourite gathering place for pensioners in the area, who used to enjoy a couple of drinks and a natter or a game of cribbage or dominoes. In the middle of 1972 the elderly tenant and his wife retired, and the pub was immediately closed for 'extensive alterations' according to the contractors notice outside. When it re-opened three months later, the public bar had been knocked through into the saloon, and the whole area covered with wall-to-wall carpeting. The tenant had been replaced by a manager who no longer kept the dominoes or the cribbage board behind the bar—nor even the darts, for this board too had been removed. The beer pumps had vanished to make way for a set of keg dispensers and all the prices were several pence up on those charged before the closure.

During the first lunchtime session after the pub re-opened, the pensioners arrived one by one to renew their old habits. They were told immediately that their custom was no longer wanted, that the pub was aiming for a different trade. In spite of a petition on their behalf signed by several hundred people, and sympathetic coverage in the local press, they have been thrown out for good. Those who can travel to other pubs in the area

do so in smaller groups: those who can't, stay at home.

This is not an isolated case. There are thousands of similar instances, many not quite so devastating to the local community, some even worse. The nature of most of the pubs that we know and have used has been changed out of all recognition in the last ten years and the bulldozer still seems to be gathering power and pace. People sit in bar corners bemoaning the declining strength and flavour of their pint. Articles about the destruction of character in old pubs appear in the press from time to time. When a tenant is given notice to quit by his brewery so that a manager can be installed, his regulars usually get up a petition. With a few exceptions, however, people have not effectively resisted the changes that have been forced upon their pubs. On the face of it, the reason could be that they do not care about these changes, even that they welcome them. Anyone who knows a pub that has been tarted up and given the gimmick treatment, or where a longstanding and popular tenant has been sacked, or where the local beer has been discontinued after a takeover, will know that this is not true. People do care greatly about what happens to their local. The problem is that where English men and women are quick to organise effectively when their home is threatened by a road scheme, or their work by a redundancy plan, they quite naturally prefer to take a more casual approach towards their leisure facilities, in the relaxed but misplaced belief that these will not be spoilt.

The growing band of environmentalists, while they are beginning to achieve so much in so many areas, have a blind spot where the pub is concerned. Its preservation should be among their highest priorities. After home and work-place most people probably spend more time in their local pub than anywhere else, more so even than the supermarket, the cinema or the local beauty spot. Some people may disapprove of this, but it is nevertheless a

10

fact. What happens to a happy spirited pub, however smoke-filled the atmosphere, and even if too much alcohol is occasionally consumed, is just as much an environmental issue as the future of Covent Garden, or what we do about pollution in the River Trent.

This is not to say that all change should be blindly resisted on the assumption that what is old is always best. Of course the pub is bound to change in some ways, and indeed needs to do so if it is to keep its vitality in the future. A great deal of money has been well spent in providing kitchen facilities so that people can have a snack as well as a pint. The standards of modern sanitation are obviously preferable to those of the nineteenth century on grounds of both hygiene and comfort. Not all old pubs are cheerful and welcoming, and those which are not can certainly benefit from a careful facelift. But items such as these account for only a small proportion of the brewers' massive spending on their tied estate. Much of this budget is used to force unwelcome change on unwilling consumers, and this is what the argument is about.

This situation has arisen because of the way the brewing industry has changed as a result of the unprecedented spate of mergers and takeovers in recent years. Fifteen years ago the industry consisted of hundreds of individual companies competing with one another locally and regionally, each producing local beers to suit local tastes. Today seven companies account for more than 80 per cent of beer sales in this country. They are: Allied Breweries, Bass Charrington, Courage, Guinness, Scottish and Newcastle, Watneys and Whitbread. Guinness is excluded from the broad scope of this book's argument, firstly because it owns no pubs, and secondly because its major product has not been reduced significantly in strength or flavour. The behaviour of the remaining companies, the 'big six' as it is convenient to call them, is the root cause of the death of the English pub. They each own several

11

thousand pubs, and partly because of their very size, have lost touch with the real needs and wants of their customers. None of them is any longer run by a brewer. They are commanded partly by marketing men, whose objectives are to banish quality and variety and to replace them with consistent mediocrity. Even the *Financial Times* has described the 'big six' as

'the major brewers whose goal is to own no more than half a dozen national brands each, all being pumped out non-stop by the most up-to-date methods available.'

The approach of the marketing men is matched by that of the accountants, who view their companies pubs as good objects for the application of their property development mentality, and refer to houses that don't fill up until nine o'clock as "redundant units."

The 'big six', of course, employ hordes of public relations men whose function is ultimately to persuade people to settle for what they don't really want. These P.R. men are given to bland generalisations about the changes that their companies are making. This approach completely misses the point because you can't generalise about pubs, the people who use them and their differing tastes in beer. That is why this book aims as far as possible to deal with individuals and small groups of people as the basis for its arguments.

When you order a pint of beer and hand over your money, you are paying for a complicated package deal. As well as the beer in your glass, the deal includes the barmaid's smile or the landlord's bonhomie, the opportunity to buy a sandwich or have a game of darts, the chance either to find a corner to chat with friends or stand at the bar and meet a stranger to the pub. In other words to enjoy the intangible but crucial feeling which is called atmosphere.

The pre-requisite of 'atmosphere' in any pub is that it should serve a good pint of beer. Writing about drink is to risk the pitfalls of pretension and pomposity, as many wine correspondents of the posh Sundays have found to their cost, and as 'Pseuds Corner' in *Private Eye* has discovered to its delight. These pitfalls are best represented by the ridiculous figure in the Thurber cartoon, who, while opening a bottle of plonk as his guests sit down for dinner at his table, announces: 'It is only a naive domestic Burgundy without any breeding but I think you'll be amused by its presumption.'

In writing about the different approaches of individual breweries and the beer they produce, I have not found it necessary to construct a league table of taste or quality. Taste varies and so, therefore, do judgements of quality. But there is one trend in the making and serving of beer that deserves to be wholeheartedly condemned. This is the application of carbon dioxide pressure to the barrel to force the beer to the point of dispense. This gas gets into the beer, putting an unpleasant tang where flavour should be, and causing acidity in the stomach. Pressurisation is alien to a well-brewed and well-kept pint of draught beer, and yet it is now the rule rather than the exception in most parts of the country. It is an innovation that is designed to cover up the weaknesses of an inferior product, served by

13

a landlord who cannot be bothered to keep his pipes clean. It is part of the trend to standardisation (rather than variety, quality, and even eccentricity of flavour) which is killing the English pub.

This trend to standardisation affects all aspects of the pub, its facilities and activities, as well as the beer itself. More and more tenants are being replaced by brewery-employed managers. The manager can be told what items to stock, while the tenant is freer to order the products his customers demand, and serve them in the way they like. The tenant furnishes his own pub, while the managed house is kitted out in fabrics and designs bought in bulk and repeated in pubs in dozens of towns. More and more small breweries are taken over each year. Local beers are discontinued and replaced with tasteless national brands. There are so many ways in which the trend to standardisation in our pubs expresses itself, and most of them are covered in subsequent chapters. Standardisation, of course, means elimination of choice and is the enemy of the distinctive but infinitely variable atmosphere that is the hallmark of the really good pub. As the major brewers have increased in size, they have become less and less accountable to the public it is their job to serve. They are already guilty, in my view, of what would elsewhere be termed robbery and violence. They have robbed the public of so many vital aspects of their leisure, and their violence has already caused the death of thousands of pubs. There are still many corners of excellence and variety in the brewing industry and the licensed trade. But if the major brewers are allowed to move with as much freedom and as little accountability in the next ten years as they have for the last ten, then the death of the English pub, which has already happened in many parts of the country, could well be accomplished everywhere.

1. The Quality of beer

'Not turning taps, but pulling pumps,
Gives barmaids splendid busts and rumps.'

Entry in a *New Statesman* competition.

'It's all piss and wind, like a barber's cat.'

Customer in a Midlands pub commenting on keg beer.

Whether it is with the elegance of a *New Statesman* reader, or with the earthiness of a public bar customer, you will find in almost every pub at least one disaffected beer drinker bemoaning the quality of his pint. Perhaps this has always been so—the tendency to believe that 'things aren't what they used to be' is deeply ingrained in many Englishmen. As far as beer is concerned, though, it is noticeable that disillusion has intensified as keg beer and 'top pressure' beer replace genuine draught beer in more and more outlets.

When you asked for a pint of bitter ten years ago it was invariably served in one of two ways: usually it would be raised from the cellar by a traditional beer engine, operated by a handle on the bar counter; occasionally it would be gravity-drawn from a barrel on or behind the bar. This beer would have arrived from the brewery in wood or metal (aluminium or stainless steel) casks, and would be required to settle in the cellar for a day or two before serving. It would not go flat because the fermentation process was still completing itself. There is no legal definition for the term 'draught beer', and afficionados argue until they are blue in the face over the precise meaning of these two words. For the purpose of this chapter, the above description is what is meant by 'draught beer'.

The simplest description of keg beer is that it is bottled beer in draught condition. The fermentation process is halted before the beer leaves the brewery by chilling, filtering and pasteurising. When the beer has been placed in its container, the residue of air is displaced by carbon dioxide, and the container is sealed for delivery. Inside the pub cellar, the container is attached to the piping, which leads to the bar, and also to a cylinder of carbon dioxide which will keep the beer under pressure and force it to the point of delivery when the tap or button is turned or pressed in the bar. Keg beer often passes through a chiller on its way to the point of dispense.

The subtle flavour of a good pint of bitter depends on the beer being relatively still and served at the right temperature. Chilled and carbonated products can never match the unique bitterness and the variety of overall palate that are available in draught beers. Resistance to keg beer has been volubly expressed in pubs for ten years or so now. The objection usually centres on the fact that keg is tasteless, insipid, too cold and too fizzy. One keg does not vary from another as draught beers do, nor does keg taste any different in one pub than in the next. Because of the equipment required to serve it, keg beer is more expensive than draught.

A report on beer in *Which* Magazine's April 1972 edition covered the controversy of draught versus keg. The principal keg and best bitter produced by each of the country's six national brewers were compared for price, alcoholic content and original gravity. The findings are shown in the opposite chart. For each brewer the keg is on the top line, the best bitter below.

In every case the draught bitter is cheaper than the keg by at least two pence. In three of the six instances the draught bitter is stronger than its rival. It is also interesting to note that with the exception of Whitbread Trophy, all four

18

		Price per Pint pence (1)	Alcohol by Volume (percent)	Original Gravity
Allied	Draught Double Diamond	15–18	3·45	1037·4°
	Ind Coope Super Draught	11–16	3·53	1036·2°
Bass Charrington	Worthington 'E'	14–18	3·98	1037·8°
	IPA Best Bitter	11–16	3·84	1039·8°
Courage	Tavern	14–18	3·82	1037·6°
	Best Bitter	12–16	4·34	1039·9°
Scottish and Newcastle	Younger's Tartan	13–17	3·71	1035·9°
	Younger's Scotch Ale	11–16	4·21	1041·3°
Watney Mann	Red	14–18	3·67	1037·9°
	Special	12–16	3·45	1036·0°
Whitbread	Tankard	14–18	3·75	1038·5°
	Trophy (2)	11–16	3·43	1034·3°

(1) Lower prices in public bars, highest in Central London (usually 2p higher than national average).
(2) South London; gravity and strength vary throughout the country.

products representing Allied Breweries and Watney Mann are weaker than any of the products representing their major competitors.

The draught beers tested by *Which* compare very favourably in price with the kegs, and hold their own as far as strength is concerned. How about taste? *Which* asked a panel of 30 people—mostly young men—to sample the kegs:

'Our tasters thought none smelled very strongly in the glass—none was either unpleasant or very pleasant. As far as taste went, the overwhelming impression of our tasters was that none of the keg beers had any very characteristic taste. None was very dry on the palate. Double Diamond tasted sweeter than the others, and Worthington 'E' less sweet.

'As well as our taste results, we also carried out a standard laboratory test for hop—bitterness. These results confirmed how similar the keg beers were. All the 'Best Bitters', except Ind Coope, gave higher bitterness figures than the keg beers. The most bitter was Bass Charrington IPA.'

On the evidence of *Which*'s sample, draught beers win hands down on price, taste, bitterness, and hold their own on strength. Whereas draught beers are (or should be) the result of the brewer's craft developed and adjusted over a period of years, often to meet the demands of varied local tastes, keg beer was dreamed up by the market research men. It provides for the average taste of the north and south, of men and women, young and old. It is beer produced according to the principle of the lowest common denominator. As such, it offends few people and satisfies even fewer. It tastes neither nice nor nasty (although there are plenty of people willing to dispute that point!) It is not surprising that as a result of their rigorous tests, *Which* came to this conclusion:

'Keg beer is a bright, chilled, fairly fizzy, moderately expensive, bland tasting beer of average strength. It should not vary very much from place to place, assuming the publican is serving it at the brewer's recommended pressures and temperatures. We can see little reason for preferring one keg bitter to another and even less for preferring them to their brewers' own alternative bitters, which are cheaper and in some cases stronger.'

The argument over the relative merits of keg and draught beer is complicated by the presence in many pubs of a third category, 'top pressure' beer. This is usually draught beer in origin, although in some cases the fermentation process will have been arrested before the barrels leave the brewery. Instead of being drawn by either of the traditional methods (gravity or the hand-pump-operated beer engine), the beer is forced to the point of dispense by carbon dioxide pressure. The drink in the customer's glass will assume the characteristics of keg according to how much of the carbon dioxide has entered

20

the beer. This, in its turn, depends on the severity of the pressure applied, which varies greatly from pub to pub. 'Top pressure' beer has a tendency to taste more like keg than draught, because it is gassy rather than still. Any subtlety of flavour in the beer will be obscured by excess carbon dioxide.

Carbon dioxide is a natural product of the fermentation process, as the brewers are quick to point out when they are criticised for the fizziness of their keg and 'top pressure' beers. The amount of carbon dioxide in a naturally brewed and traditionally served pint is known in the industry as the 'one to one ratio'. When such a pint goes flat, it is of course because it has lost all or part of its natural carbon dioxide content. If you ordered a pint of draught beer, stood it on the bar to let it go flat, and trapped the carbon dioxide given off, the gas you had collected would just about fill a pint pot. This what is meant by the 'one to one ratio'. With 'top pressure' and keg beers, the gas side of the ratio increases.

Where the 'top pressure' is relatively gentle, the increase may only be to 1·1:1. With a heavily carbonated keg beer, it can be upwards of 1·5:1. The actual figures are not important to the beer drinker. What matters is that the balance of his pint is disturbed. As carbonation is induced, so flavour is lost. It is also easier to sustain excess levels of carbonation if the beer is cold, and this is one reason why so many 'top pressure' and keg beers are heavily chilled when they reach your glass.

With beers whose taste is governed by coldness and fizziness, it becomes less important for the brewers to use good quality malt and hops, because the body and the bitterness that these products contribute cannot be detected anyway. The amount of malt substitute used in the industry is on the increase. Typical examples are rice and maize, either flaked or in grits. Instead of whole hops, oils, powders and substitutes are increasingly being used.

21

In 1961, only 112 cwt. of hop preparations and substitutes were used in the brewing industry. By 1969 this had risen steadily to 1609 cwt, and jumped dramatically to 6044 cwt. in 1970. Every year the amount of substitutes for real malt and hops used by the brewing industry increases, not only in total but also in proportion. The head brewer of a sizeable family firm which has resisted the temptation to cheapen its products in this way, spoke out recently against the trend to what he called 'chemical engineering'.

There is no doubt in the minds of millions of drinkers, of journalists who have researched the public's taste, of dissenters within the brewing industry itself, that keg is an inferior product to genuine draught beer. Yet more keg is sold each year, and its share of the beer market increases steadily. Keg accounted for just 1% of beer sales in 1959. By 1965 it was taking 7% of the market, and 18% by 1971.

There are two principal reasons why an inferior drink has been able to capture such a large share of the market. Firstly, genuine draught beer is no longer available in thousands of pubs. The bitter drinker is often restricted to a choice between keg or 'top pressure' products. 'Top pressure' beer is usually a hybrid, brewed as draught, served as keg. It has the disadvantages of both, the advantages of neither. The request for a pint of keg is often a reflection of the lack of a genuine alternative, pointing to deficient supply rather than to positive demand. Not only an individual pub, but complete districts, sometimes whole towns, may suffer from a deficient supply situation, particularly where two or three national brewers own all the outlets and are pursuing identical policies.

Secondly, the brewers' advertising is dedicated almost entirely to the promotion of keg rather than draught beers. Double Diamond, Worthington 'E', Courage Tavern, Watneys Red, Youngers Tartan, Whitbread Tankard— these are what the big six want to sell, and these are what they advertise. The reason is simple. The *Financial*

Times estimated recently that the brewers' profit margin on kegs and lagers (which are also advertised heavily) is approximately 50% more than on draught beer. The incessant advertising of the last ten years has had its effect, particularly on the two sectors of society who have come to use pubs and spend substantial amounts of money in them during that period—young people and women.

Commenting on the brewers' claim that the increase in keg sales indicated public acceptance of an innovation, Graham Bannock, the economist, wrote in his recent book, *The Juggernauts**:

'More probably it simply reflects the exercise of marketing power. Most of the brewers' draught beer advertising is now entirely devoted to keg and it is impossible to get anything else in many pubs . . . Without tied sales outlets and without heavy selective advertising it is most unlikely that keg beers could have been introduced on anything like the scale so far achieved. As it is, the Juggernaut brewers will soon be in a position to abolish cask beer altogether, although it will no doubt be attributed to the power of the market.'

Thankfully, many local and regional brewers have chosen not to follow the same course as their national competitors. Greene King, of Bury St. Edmunds, is one of the largest independent regional brewers. The company took a policy decision some years ago to stick with traditional products rather than jump on the keg bandwaggon. In 1971, the Managing Director was able to report that the policy was paying off and that record sales had been achieved during the previous year. In his report to the company's shareholders he explained:

'The quality of our beers is excellent, and in particular our real draught beer is growing in popularity in competition with the so called premium keg beers of some of our competitors. As most drinkers know, traditional draught beer has more character and flavour than filtered and pasteurised keg beer and is generally cheaper too.'

A small company in Selby, Yorkshire, closed down its brewing operations in the 1950s. As the national brewers moved into the town, the quality of Selby's beer rapidly deteriorated. The company's workers, engaged in other activities now, were constantly being stopped in the

The Juggernauts, Graham Bannock, Weidenfeld, 1971.

streets, challenged in the pubs, by people asking them to start brewing again. After carefully gauging local demand, the management decided to restore the brewing side of the company's operations. The Selby Brewery re-opened in 1972. Manager John Braithwaite commented on the local beer market and the gap in demand he hoped to fill:

'Many people told us they were getting a bit sick of the keg and other beers. The public seems to have rebelled against the red revolution and the fistful of flavour firms. People tell us that keg beers are insipid copies of the real thing—beer straight from a wooden barrel.'

Publicans too, have encountered the same rebellion. Robert Watson, landlord of the Rose and Crown, a free house at Princes Risborough, Buckinghamshire, installed keg beer in 1961. By 1966 his customers were complaining vehemently and trade was falling off. 'Sales have dropped,' he said at the time. 'I find keg only suits the brewers and doesn't do me any good at all. It is too impersonal, and hasn't any individuality.' He ripped out the keg equipment and reverted to selling draught beer, to the benefit of both his customers and himself. The tenants and managers of tied houses do not, unfortunately, have the option of meeting local demand in this way.

The beer-drinker who feels strongly about the declining quality of his pint has two organisations he can turn to, both of which are contesting a wide range of issues on his behalf—the long-established Society for the Preservation of Beers from the Wood, and the more recently formed, more militant CAMRA (Campaign for Real Ale).

In October 1963, a letter from a disgruntled bitter drinker was published in the *Financial Times*. It was a forceful statement of the widely-felt consternation of bitter drinkers at the increasing use of carbon dioxide as a means of keeping and serving beer in pubs and clubs. The ensuing correspondence was discussed one evening at the Rising Sun in Epsom by seven regulars—later to become the inaugural members of the Society for the Preservation of Beers from the Wood. One of the seven, Arthur Millard, is now the Society's President. A retired City banker, usually a mild-mannered man, he is anything but gentle when he looks back on the treatment that brewers have given the public. He recalls the situation when the Society was formed in 1963, when keg was little more than an innovation:

'Even then, everyone concerned—drinkers, brewers, publicans —we were all aware that keg was inordinately expensive and didn't deserve the name of bitter. Its taste was unpleasant as a result of the lethal treatment it received at the hands of the brewers in the first place. Here was nothing less than a gassed-up dead liquid as opposed to a live, working beer. It was fobbed off on the public, in the sacred name of hygiene and purity. The landlord's skill in keeping his beer engines in good repair, in keeping his pipes clean, became redundant overnight. Keg requires no skill to keep. Any ignoramus with a spanner can stock and serve it.'

Membership of the Society grew rapidly, branches were formed in different parts of the country. A tie was designed and produced for members, displaying a number of wooden casks on a black background, implying mourning for the passing of real draught beer. The social rather than activist side of the Society was uppermost in the early period. The *Daily Mail* described the Society at this time as 'a bit of a giggle with serious undertones'. Members probably under-estimated the scale and the imminence of the threat with which their beer was faced.

When the Society was formed nine years ago, its title was relevant—beer drawn straight from wooden barrels was still widely available. Wooden casks disappeared all over the country during the mid 1960s, and were replaced by metal barrels made either from aluminium or stainless steel. A debate racked the Society for some years as to whether these new barrels should be approved. It was finally decided that while wooden barrels would always be preferred, metal would be accepted, and that the main issue to be contested was the way that beer was served. Pressurisation became the target. Arthur Millard is as contemptuous of 'top pressure' as of keg beer. He told me,

'I went into a pub just after opening time some weeks ago. One of the first customers asked for a pint which was dispensed by 'top pressure.' It took the barman eight minutes to serve it. The stuff was spuming all over the place. "It'll be all right by seven o'clock, sir," was all he could say.'

No fee is charged for membership of the Society, whose headquarters are at Ye Old Watling, Watling Street, in the City of London. Prospective members are asked to name their local, which has to be approved by the Society. They are also asked to sign two pledges—firstly, 'to stimulate the brewing and to encourage the drinking of beers drawn from the wood'; secondly 'to denigrate the manufacture and sale of beer in 'sealed dustbins' (keg beer) and to discourage its consumption.' The recruitment policy is a passive one; the Society does not approach people, it waits to be approached. Membership has nevertheléss grown to 2500, and many of the new members are bringing a more militant attitude into the Society. This is reflected in some of the activities of the last couple of years.

Trumans produced a draught beer that was much favoured by members of the Society in London and the south-east until recently when the company ceased brewing in Burton and simultaneously went over to the top pressure method of dispense in the vast majority of their pubs. A wreath was taken to the London Stone and placed over the last barrel of the real stuff. At the aptly named Who'd 'a Thought It, a mock funeral service was held. A thirty-six gallon barrel was interred in the back garden of the pub by the local branch chairman, dressed up as a vicar. Very few members visit Trumans pubs these days!

In 1971 the Society petitioned the Department of Trade

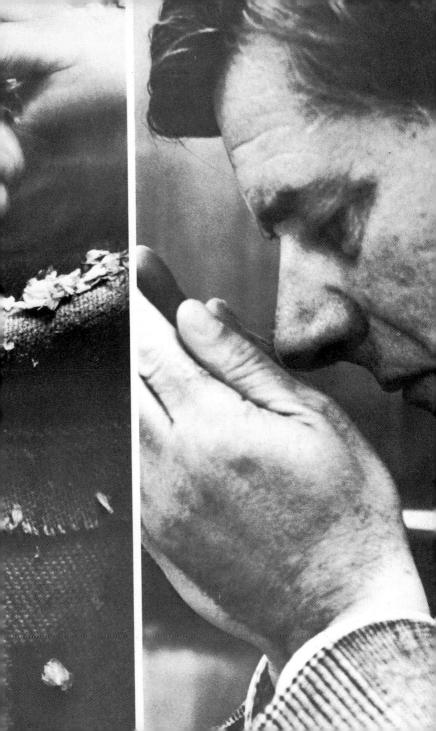

and Industry in an attempt to secure legal definitions under the Trade Descriptions Act for the terms 'keg', 'top pressure', and 'draught' in relation to beer. This would have prevented brewers from confusing the public by a misleading and inconsistent use of terminology. Unfortunately, the Society was unsuccessful in achieving this objective. Many members within the organisation, and sympathisers without, are dissatisfied with the Society's general lack of a campaigning approach, and its lack of success when it does campaign. It was this vacuum which the founders of C A M R A hoped to fill when they formed their rival organisation in 1971.

C A M R A is the brainchild of a group of young men from the north-west, some of whom had come to work in London and the south-east. They were appalled by the high prices, low standards of service, and above all by the lack of choice and the poor quality of beer in London's pubs. Michael Hardman, one of the leading members of the campaign, says:

'I'd never thought about my beer too much until I came to live down here. I'd always been used to a good pint in friendly surroundings without having to take too much trouble to find it. I was shocked by the state of affairs in London when I first arrived. Of course, there are good pubs and good beer in this area, just as good as in the north. But there are fewer of them and they're harder to find.'

This experience is reflected in the campaign's approach, which is based on keeping its members informed about good beer and where to find it as well as on fighting the spread of keg and top pressure beers. A monthly newsheet is mailed to all members. It covers local issues, broader trends in the industry, in addition to the campaign's activities. A list of several hundred pubs in all parts of the country that serve real draught beer has been published— a kind of good pub guide, but with the accent on beer rather than amenity or food.

CAMRA is just as violent in its opposition to keg and other pressurised beers as the Society for the Preservation of Beers from the Wood. A series of articles has been running in the campaign's newsheet, *What's Brewing*, under the heading 'The Polluted Pint'. It aims to expose the ways in which the brewers set out to confuse their customers into an acceptance of beer of an inferior quality. Deception in pubs, too, is among the campaign's targets. Dirty Dick's in Bishopsgate, one of London's best-known pubs, was serving beer which apparently came straight from huge wooden barrels situated behind the bar. Customers were being given the impression that they were getting 'Draught Bass from the Wood'. In fact, pipes led from the taps through the hollow barrels and down to the cellar where they were connected to pressurised metal barrels. In order to avoid prosecution under the Trade Descriptions Act, Dirty Dick's agreed to display notices explaining that the beer was served under pressure.

Perhaps CAMRA's most ambitious project to date is the detailed report dispatched during the Autumn, 1973, to all Members of Parliament, many of whom are already known to be sympathetic to the campaign's objectives. Michael Hardman believes that beer drinkers get a raw deal in terms of legal protection:

'CAMRA has for some time been of the opinion that legislation is needed to force brewers and pubs into admitting just what they sell. We believe that all beer should be sold with labels— either on the bottle or on the pump—giving information about alcoholic content, original gravity, method and place of brewing, and in the case of draught, or so-called draught beer, the means by which it is drawn from the barrel, cask or keg. We aim to convince Parliament of the need for this kind of consumer protection and we know that there are many MPs who are as concerned about the situation as we are.'

In the meantime, support for CAMRA is growing. CAMRA, which operates from 207 Keats Court, Salford,

Lancashire, has a more active approach to recruitment and is less restrictive in its terms of membership than the Society for the Preservation of Beers from the Wood, although there is an annual fee of 50 pence. A network of area organisers covering the country is encouraged to sign up new members, who are admitted to the campaign as long as they have a preference for real draught beer rather than keg and top pressure products.

It may be that both of these organisations need to adopt a harder, more professional approach and to be able to draw on greater funds and expertise, if they are to attract massive support in the country and make a significant impact on the activities of the big brewers. But there is little doubt that they have a good case, whether they succeed in winning it or not. If further proof of this is required it was given to me by a member of one of these organisations. He showed me the results of the competitions held at the 1972 Brewers Exhibition. In the draught beer contest, there were seventeen prizes; sixteen went to local and regional brewers, one to the big six. Twenty three awards were made in the bottled beer competition; twenty one to the smaller companies, two to the nationals. Even in the keg section, all three prizes went to little known companies. The big six brewers produce 70% of the country's beer. In open competition with the smaller breweries, they won 5% of the prizes at the 1972 Brewers Exhibition. Over the last ten years the big six may have learnt all there is to know about market research, about takeover bids, about public relations. In the process one of two things appears to have happened. Either they have forgotten how to brew good beer, or they have decided not to bother any more.

2. The Strength of beer

'I contend that there is something idiotic in a situation in which a retailer can be prosecuted for watering down beer, but the brewer can, in effect, do the same thing with impunity to his own financial advantage.'

GEOFFREY RHODES MP

There is a drinking song that includes the following verse:

> I'm the man, the very fat man,
> That waters the workers' beer,
> What do I care if it makes them ill,
> If it makes them horribly queer—
> I've a car, a yacht, and an aeroplane.
> And I waters the workers' beer.

Unscrupulous landlords down the ages have watered the beer they serve, and prosecutions for this offence are still brought from time to time. The watering of beer is, however, a method of adulteration that has become more sophisticated in recent years. Today it happens in the brewery rather than in the cellar of the pub. For years, the beer we drink has been getting weaker, which means, among other things, that it has more water and less alcohol in it. The brewers, with a few notable exceptions, are quite literally watering the workers' beer.

Original gravity, known in the industry as O.G., is the measurement of beer according to which the Excise Authority calculates the duty payable. The majority of British beers have an O.G. of between $1030°$ and $1050°$, although there are exceptions outside both ends of this range. Original gravity is a measurement of the quantities of materials used in a brew, and is taken before fermentation. Beer is made

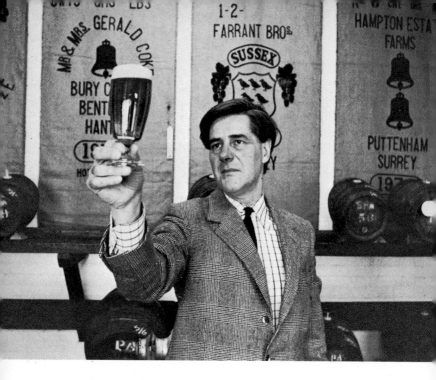

by fermenting a solution of sugars extracted from malt. 100 gallons of water weighs 1000 lbs., so if 100 gallons of sugar solution weighs 1045 lbs. the original gravity is said to be 1045°.

During fermentation the dissolved sugars are converted into alcohol and carbon dioxide by the addition of yeast. It follows that the more sugar there is in the solution (or, in other words, the higher the original gravity), the greater is the alcoholic content of the beer that *can* be brewed from it. Original gravity, therefore, is a measurement of the potential strength of a beer before fermentation, not its actual strength afterwards.

Given a certain original gravity, the actual strength of a beer (its alcoholic content), is dictated by the extent to which the fermentation process is allowed to continue or how much of the sugar is converted and how much left. The term 'attenuation' refers to the loss of material during the fermentation process through residue, frothing, and the giving off of carbon dioxide. It is usual for the amount by which the weight of the brew exceeds the weight of an equivalent amount of water to be attenuated by between 65% and 80% during fermentation. The average figure for the British brewing industry is approximately 75%. (There are, of course, brews whose attenuation rate falls outside this 65%–80% range. They tend to taste extremely nasty. If the fermentation process is halted too soon the beer will resemble syrup, or if too late, it will be more like vinegar. These extremes were best described by *The London and Country Brewing Book*, an eighteenth century manual, which referred to them respectively as 'thick, groutish, fickish, fulsome Ale,' and 'sharp, harsh or ill-tasting Beer.')

An original gravity of, say, 1048°, will be reduced by fermentation to a final gravity of 1012°, if the average rate of attenuation (75%) applies. The percentage of alcohol in the finished beer can be roughly obtained by dividing the difference between the original and the final gravity (in this case thirty-six) by the figure of eight. This particular beer therefore, would have an alcoholic content of approximately $4\frac{1}{2}$% by volume.

It may be thought that these processes and calculations are best left to the head brewers. This would be true, except for the fact that they are no longer to be trusted. They have been using the complexities of their craft to weaken the beer we drink while denying that this is what they are doing. The brewers are fond of pointing out that original gravity has no direct relationship with alcoholic strength. This is true in a strict sense, but nevertheless misleading. Original gravity does have an indirect relationship with alcoholic strength that provides a pretty good rule of thumb guide. This is that the higher the original gravity of a brew, the greater the alcoholic strength of the finished beer is likely to be.

The reason for the brewers' propaganda is that they have been reducing the original gravity of the country's beer, and would prefer their customers to remain ignorant of the implications of this trend. They have not been too successful in this respect. While the beer·drinker may not be aware of the ins and outs of gravity, attenuation, and so on, he certainly realises that the brew he is offered today is weaker even than that of a few years ago. After Lord Stonham had described the watering of beer as a 'large-scale swindle' in the House of Lords in 1971, the London *Evening News* took to the city's bars to find out if beer drinkers agreed. 'Strong words', wrote their reporter, 'but as I soon found out the sentiments they express are almost unanimously shared by London beer drinkers.' One sixty-three year old gentleman made his point forcefully and with the perspective of forty-five years' beer drinking to back him up. He had switched from bitter to bottled stout ten years previously, and told the reporter:

'It was at that time that I realised that the beer really was being watered down. The brewers were getting away with robbery then, and now they're getting away with blue murder. They've gone on putting the price up while at the same time taking the strength out of their beer. In the old days when you'd had three pints you'd had enough but you could go on drinking pints all night nowadays and still be almost as sober as when you came in . . .'

It is not hard to find the reason behind the watering of Britain's beer. The rates of excise duty are graded according to a beer's original gravity. Until the intro-duction of VAT in April 1973 the payment due on a standard barrel (36 gallons) with an O.G. of 1030° was £10.37½ pence. Each additional degree of gravity incurred an incremental levy of 44 pence. The duty pay-able on a standard barrel with an O.G. of 1035° was £12.57½ pence; if the O.G. were raised to 1045°, the duty increased to £16.97½ pence, a difference of £4.40p. Thus substantial savings could be made on a single barrel of beer if the original gravity was reduced. The

brewing industry produces upwards of thirty million barrels a year. The enormous potential for brewers to increase their profits by weakening their beers becomes evident.

To accommodate the introduction of VAT at the 10% rate, the brewers' excise liability was reduced by approximately one third. The standard rate of £10.37½ pence per barrel was reduced to £6.90 pence, and the rate per additional degree of gravity came down from 44 pence to 29 pence. The brewers can still effect savings by reducing the strength of their beers, although the amount of these savings is not now so great. But all that VAT has done is to close part of the stable door after most of the horses have bolted.

The average gravity of the UK's beer has been declining for the last decade. The last year in which it rose was 1964 when it went up to 1037.43° from 1037.41° in 1963. Since then, according to the Annual Report of the Customs and Excise Department, the figures have been as follows:

1964	1037.43°	1968	1036.93°
1965	1037.41°	1969	1036.78°
1966	1037.26°	1970	1036.65°
1967	1037.15°		

These reductions in strength may seem minuscule, but the financial implications are not. If the beer consumed in 1970 had been brewed at the strength that prevailed in 1964, the additional cost to the brewing industry would have been in the region of £11M. That £11M is, in effect, a hidden price increase, paid by the beer drinker, because the brewers do not tell us when they weaken their products, and they do not lower their prices accordingly.

It is worth noting that the average gravity of beer in 1970 is the lowest ever figure except during the Second World War and its immediate aftermath, when the raw materials needed for the brewing process were in scarce supply.* In fact, the grim situation evident from the Customs and Excise Department's statistics understates the real trend. Final alcoholic content (on which, unfortunately, there are no offical statistics) is more important to the beer drinker than original gravity. In recent years, the switch to keg beers would have meant that beer was getting weaker even if the original gravity had remained the same. For keg products, which are achieving an increasing hold on the beer market, the fermentation process is arrested before the beer leaves the brewery, and less alcohol accrues in the finished beer. A greater proportion of unfermented sugar remains in the barrel, which makes the beer sweeter, and gives the impression of greater strength than is really the case.

Average figures for the entire industry do not, of course, reflect the fact that while some brewers have kept faith with their customers and maintained the strength of their beers, others have been involved in making savage reductions both to the original gravity and acoholic content of certain selected brands. Often it is the national brewers who are most to blame. Often, too, the biggest reductions in strength have been effected in those products which have the highest sales volumes, thus maximising the incremental profit. The enormous promotional budgets which sustain and increase the sales of many national brands by persuading drinkers that they are buying a good, strong pint, are sometimes paid for times over by the weakening of the brew whose strength they vaunt.

It is a great pity that no consumer organisation has regularly tested the strength of a large number of beers over the last ten years. The wide publication of reductions in original gravity might have persuaded some brewers to discontinue the policy of gradually weakening their products. Some excellent work has been done on the

*In 1971 the O.G. of the UK's beer rose for the first time in seven years – by 0·03°!

subject, principally by the Consumers' Association through *Which* magazine, and by the *Mirror* Group of newspapers, each of whom has published two detailed reports on the subject. The first investigation by the Consumers' Association appeared in *Which* in 1960. The three more recent reports were published by the *Sunday Mirror* (March 1971), *Which* (April 1972), and the *Daily Mirror* (July 1972). These three reports checked on a number of beers that were originally tested in the 1960 investigation. Some of the results are startling.

According to *Which* in 1960, Watneys Special Bitter had an original gravity of $1043.1°$. In March 1971 the *Sunday Mirror* found that this had dropped to $1037.9°$. If these figures are correct (and there is no reason to assume otherwise, as they have never been contested by the brewers concerned), each barrel of Watneys Special Bitter brewed at its 1971 gravity was costing the company £2.64 pence per barrel less in excise duty than if its strength had been maintained. In April 1972 *Which* tested the same brew again, and the original gravity was $1036.0°$, a further saving of 44 pence per barrel. In 1960, Worthington 'E' was found to have an original gravity of $1041.8°$. The *Sunday Mirror* re-checked on this in 1971 and the new figure was $1036.8°$. Ansell's bitter (produced by the Midland subsidiary of Allied Breweries) came down from $1045.3°$ in 1960 to $1038.9°$ by 1971. There are other examples too numerous to mention, but the general picture has already emerged. These savings per barrel in excise duty should be viewed in relation to the fact that the sales of the country's top beer brands can exceed half a million barrels per annum. It is only fair to mention at this stage, that while the figures produced by the Consumers' Association and the two *Mirror* newspapers show the activities of most of the national brewers in a highly unfavourable light, there are two notable exceptions. The evidence suggests that, unlike their major competitors, Courage

41

and Scottish and Newcastle have maintained the strength of their beers.

Apart from these comparisons with the *Which* report of 1960, the more recent investigations have reached some staggering conclusions about other brands of beer on sale today. The *Sunday Mirror* found in 1971 that, among others, the following beers were so weak that they could have been legally sold in the United States during the era of prohibition: Ind Coope Superdraught, Whitbread Starbright, Ansell's Kingpin Keg, Watneys Starlight, Watneys Special Mild. Peter Seeds, the *Sunday Mirror's* investigator had this to say of the weakest draught beer tested:

'Watneys Special Mild, apart from having the least alcohol in it, also propped up the pile with an O.G. rating of 1030·4°. This brew is so weak that if it dropped in strength by about one per cent of alcohol, it would be classed as "near beer" and could be sold to children as a mineral water.'

Returning to the attack in 1972, Richard Seear of the *Daily Mirror* singled out the lager category of draught beers for testing. He was forced to the conclusion on draught Carlsberg and Tuborg (marketed in this country by Watneys and Trumans respectively) that:

'We think these two lagers more suitable for a maiden aunt of moderate habits than a man who uses his muscles.'

In this as in many other respects, some of the smaller brewers have kept the faith with their customers that their larger competitors have arrogantly decided they can do without. Fair dealing may be a concept that is stone dead in the minds of the accountants who have seized control of large sectors of the industry, but it survives elsewhere as an example. In October 1971, Youngs of Wandsworth replaced their existing light ale and barley wine by two new brands, Ram Rod and Old Nick. The new light ale

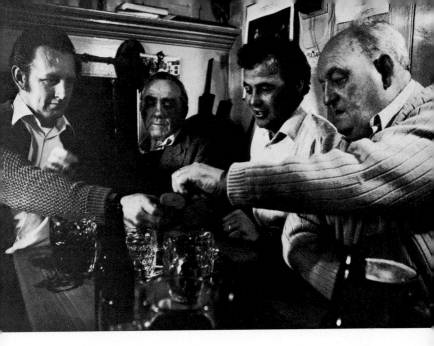

was 2° higher in gravity than its predecessor, the new barley wine 5° higher. The company's chairman, John Young, explains:

'In the past, as well as preserving the quality of our products, we have tried to keep them a little bit cheaper than those of our competitors. When public bar prices were de-controlled in 1970, our tenants quite understandably adjusted their prices to the levels charged in nearby pubs. We decided the advantages of the new situation should be divided three ways. Our wholesale margins and our tenants' retail margins are slightly higher, and our customers get a stronger and better drink.'

More recently, the gravity of Young's successful Saxon Lager has also been increased.

Heartening as this example (and there are probably one or two others like it) may be, the overall trend appears to be inexorable. Beer is getting weaker year by year. If this pattern continues many nationally known brands will soon be able to take their place on sweet-shop shelves, alongside the lemonade and the dandelion and burdock.

The principal reason for the weakening of our beer is that certain brewers have found they can increase their profits substantially with the aid of a watering can. This is not the first time the brewers have been criticised for this process, and their response is likely to be the same as on previous occasions. They have always reacted by saying that a consumer's preference for one beer against another does not depend primarily on strength, but more on taste, appearance and so on. This may well be true, but it misses the real point. When the brewer weakens a particular beer, he is not obliged to reveal the fact, nor is he obliged to reduce his prices. In fact he never does either of these things. Yet his customer is getting less for his money, is paying a hidden price increase. When the housewife buys a tin of peas or a packet of sugar, the weight is clearly marked. When the spirits drinker buys a bottle of whisky or gin, he knows the strength, or proof, of what he's getting. The pub-goer has remained unprotected for too long against the watering of his beer.

3. The Choice of beer

'A glass of bitter, however excellent, can't compare with a premier cru claret. But beer is all we have and deliberately to destroy most of the places where good beer is brewed is a national loss whichever way you look at it.'

DEREK COOPER in *The Beverage Report*

Bass Charrington are currently building the largest brewery in Europe at Runcorn New Town. The cost will be approximately £25M and the brewery will be capable of producing over 700 million pints of beer each year, a twelfth of the country's entire supply. This development involves the certain closure of eight local and regional breweries belonging to Bass Charrington. Five are in Lancashire, at Barrow, Blackpool, Burnley, Liverpool and Manchester. Two are in South Wales—Aberbeeg and Fernvale. The eighth is at Mile End in London. It is possible, too, that the company's Sheffield brewery will close down as well. When this rationalisation is completed, Bass Charrington will have no brewery further south than Birmingham.

Bass Charrington's senior management are proud of what they believe to be a bold and imaginative re-organisation of their company's affairs. The shareholders, too, hope to benefit from the even greater profits which are expected to accrue. The people who will lose out when Runcorn opens and the other breweries close, are many of the men and women who work for Bass Charrington in Lancashire, London and South Wales; and also the company's customers. The breweries at Burnley and Aberbeeg for example may not be very big, or very modern, but they produce beers which suit the palate of the local people.

This is something that computerised, push-button super breweries are incapable of doing. Similar developments by Bass Charrington's competitors have shown that most new breweries are invariably used to produce a restricted range of national brands that sell into the vacuum created by the closure of local breweries. Local tastes and preferences are over-ridden. Drinkers either learn to gulp and swallow the new and more expensive brands offered to them or they stay at home. A variety of excellent, traditional products are wiped out overnight. The consumer's choice is impoverished irreparably.

The number of breweries producing Britain's beer is decreasing rapidly. The Customs and Excise department issues a permit to brew and sell to each brewery each year. The numbers of these 'Brewers for Sale Licenses' that have been granted are as follows:

1920	2914	1964	295
1930	1418	1965	274
1940	840	1966	246
1950	567	1967	243
1960	358	1968	231
1961	336	1969	210
1962	317	1970	176
1963	304		

No one could seriously argue for a return to the 1920 situation, when each town had several independent breweries, and hundreds of pubs brewed their own beer. But the trend is clear and disturbing. In every decade since the First World War, a half or nearly a half of the country's breweries have been closed down. Between 1960 and 1970 the average number of closures was eighteen yearly, and the rate increased steadily after 1967. The 176 breweries that remained in 1970 were owned by less than 100 separate companies. If takeovers, mergers, and the subsequent brewery closures are allowed to continue on the recent scale it seems likely that any real choice the consumer still enjoys will have been eradicated by 1980. The big six brewers have already shown a feverish anxiety to withdraw popular local products from the market and replace them with national brands.

There is an area on the borders of Sussex and Surrey where a wide selection of good beers used to be obtainable. Hilaire Belloc wrote of these districts:

> They Sell good Beer at Haslemere
>   And under Guildford Hill.
> At Little Cowfold as I've been told
>   A beggar may drink his fill:
> There is a good brew in Amberley too,
>   And by the bridge also;
> But the swipes they take in at Washington Inn
>   Is the very best Beer I know.

In the 1950s Watneys took over two Sussex breweries and soon decided to discontinue the separate draught bitters produced by these companies. A hybrid brew called 'Sussex bitter' was introduced. According to many local people it was inferior to both of the brews it replaced, but better than any of Watneys national brands, Red, Special and Starlight. Early in 1970, Sussex bitter was withdrawn from the market and replaced by Watneys Special. The Chairman of Watneys' regional subsidiary explained:

'We are sorry to see Sussex bitter go, but tastes change. The decision to discontinue this beer has not been taken lightly but its sales have not been buoyant and have lately been falling steadily; at the same time, sales of Watneys Special Bitter have been growing fast throughout the south of England.'

'We have, therefore, come to the conclusion that the best way to satisfy our customers is to extend the availability of this national beer which has been in many of our houses for some months and for which we forecast an even greater demand. Where a need for a lower priced bitter develops, Starlight will be made available.'

49

There were two principal reasons why sales of Sussex bitter fell prior to its withdrawal from the market. Firstly, Watney representatives had been pressing their tenants to take Special rather than Sussex bitter for months, and had succeeded in some cases. Secondly, Watneys had been refusing to supply Sussex bitter to some of the pubs that wanted to order it. This point was made by Terry Aspinall, a Worthing licensee, in a speech he made to a local branch of the Licensed Victuallers' Association:

'I understand the brewery ceased delivery of Sussex bitter to many smaller houses because, they said, quantities involved did not merit delivery. This would of itself result in less sales though it would not prove that public demand had fallen off. It would simply mean fewer people could get it at the house of their choice.'

When brewers present 'falling demand' as the reason for withdrawing a popular local product, they are often asking the public to believe the same fallacy that is so succinctly exposed in this licensee's speech.

Ten years or so after their takeovers in Sussex, Watneys bought up Steward and Patteson and Bullards. Both companies brewed in Norwich and provided much of East Anglia's beer. Three months after Sussex bitter was withdrawn from the market, Norwich bitter was launched, replacing the separate beers hitherto produced by Steward and Patteson and Bullards. Norwich bitter is yet another hybrid neutral beer that has little of the characteristic flavour of the products it replaced. While many of the local people do not like it much, and protested vigorously over the disappearance of their favourite brews, they find it better than nothing at all, and slightly better than Special or Starlight. When Norwich bitter was launched, Giles Myrtle, an executive of Watneys' regional company, claimed:

'This re-affirms our promise to retain local beers to satisfy local tastes while there is a reasonable demand.'

50

STEWARD & PATTESON L.TD.

CAT & FIDDLE

How long will it be before the Sussex pattern is repeated in Norwich? Even if this pledge is kept, the real choice that the customer had between a pint of Steward and Patteson and a pint of Bullards has already been lost.

A peculiarly inverted sense of logic prompted Giles Myrtle to claim that the replacement of two beers by one meant that East Anglian drinkers now had the widest selection of draught beers ever to choose from!

It would have been more accurate of him to point out that his company's customers had just been deprived of one of the last elements of a choice that had been very wide as recently as the early 1950s. At that time there were six brewers in Norfolk, each producing a minimum of two and an average of three draught beers. Five of these brewers were swallowed at first or second hand by Watneys, the sixth by Whitbread. The result of these takeovers is that where there were six separate companies, now there are two; where there were seven breweries functioning in the county, now there is one; where there were at least eighteen local draught beers, now there is one, plus a handful of national brands. When, in spite of facts like these, brewers blandly assure their customers that variety and choice are increasing, the extent to which the truth is being bent to the requirements of public relations becomes clear.

Watneys are by no means the only offenders in refusing to supply the beer the public wants. In 1970, Bass Charrington launched Brew X, a new draught bitter, in the north of England. Frank Barlow, landlord of the Parkinsons Arms, Scunthorpe, was informed that he would have to take Brew X instead of Stones bitter, which is produced by Bass Charrington's Sheffield brewery, as it was no longer intended to deliver the latter further than ten miles south of Sheffield. Frank Barlow's customers were so dismayed by the threatened substitution that he offered to collect his beer from the brewery, but Bass Charrington still refused. 'It is not true that Stones is being discontinued, merely that Brew X is being promoted,' a brewery spokesman was reported as saying.

At much the same time, Courage launched their Full Brew in Bristol and the west country, and in some pubs the ordinary bitter was withdrawn. Michael Cocks, the M.P. for Bristol South, was so disturbed by the implications of this move, that he decided to raise the matter in the House of Commons. His speech, made in April 1971, is worth quoting at some length:

'Of the 50 public houses in my constituency in Bristol 47 are controlled by Courages,* as I have found from looking through the records of the magistrates' courts. That is pretty nearly a monopoly. After the war, in Bristol, there were some small local breweries, Georges and United, but a series of takeovers occurred and in the end seemed to be dominated not so much by Bristol's interests as by London's interests. For a long time Bristol has been known as a city where a comparatively cheap pint of bitter was available. Many people enjoy a drink, including many old people for whom it is an important part of their social life.

'Last year, advertisements began to appear in the local newspapers advertising a new beer by Courages—Full Brew. It was called "the regular's bitter". The advertisements showed three glasses and at the top were the words "Same again, Frank?" "Same again, Bert." I presume that using those names was some ad-man's idea of a working class image. . . .

'Not surprisingly, this is a more expensive beer than the ordinary bitter, the "cooking bitter", which is the general drink in Bristol. A number of my constituents were worried about this and some of them got in touch with me because they feared that the brewery was trying to persuade the general public to accept this more expensive bitter in place of the cheaper ordinary bitter to which they had become accustomed.

'I was concerned because the more expensive price would obviously hit those of limited means who enjoyed a quiet drink. Someone wrote to the *Evening Post*, the local newspaper point-

*A number of Courage houses in Bristol have since been exchanged for Watney pubs in Brighton, Northampton and Norwich.

ing out that in her local the ordinary bitter had been withdrawn and that only this more expensive beer was available—apart from the other keg beers and so on. There was a reply from a brewery spokesman to say that there was another house nearby where the cheaper beer was available.

'This was a bad answer, because it completely ignored the fact that elderly people get accustomed to going to one house over many years and they build up social contacts. If they are then told that if they go down the road to another house, their beer will be two pence a pint cheaper, the way in which they have woven their local into the fabric of their life is completely ignored . . .

If the withdrawal of popular local beers by the big six has the effect of seriously reducing the consumer's choice, the impact of takeovers and mergers on product variety is devastating. A map of London and south-eastern breweries was published in 1951. It is worth listing those companies that have fallen under the hammer in the last twenty years. Breweries outside London are only listed if they had pubs in the capital itself:

London	*Reading*
Barclay Perkins	Higgs
C. Beasley	Simond
Cannon Brewery	
Fremlins	*Watford*
Hammerton	Benskins
Harmans	Wells
Lovibond	
Mann Crossman and Paulin	*Bexley*
Meux	Reffells
South London	
Taylor Walker	*Wateringbury*
Wenlock Brewery	Leney
Edmund Woodhead	
	Guildford
	Friary

Twenty breweries in one area, providing an enormous range of choice, and all of them shut in twenty years. There are only two local breweries left in London now, Fuller Smith and Turner at Chiswick, Youngs at Wands-

worth. Even in the country's biggest market, where minority products might be expected to last longest, the range of beers on sale has been decimated since the last war.

'The public has got to learn to like it.' That is almost true, but not quite. In most regions of the country, there are a handful of independent brewers who continue to brew traditional beers, in response to public demand. If many more of these companies are the victims of takeovers and mergers, not only will their beers be lost, all trace of genuine competition in the industry will vanish. There will be no standard against which the increasingly insipid new products of the big six can be judged.

4. The Big Six

'The public are at the brewers' mercy.'

JOHN BIGGS-DAVISON, right-wing Conservative M.P.

'You are not dealing with brewers today. They look on your houses as profitable building sites. Don't be complacent and think that things will get better. They will get worse. Maxwell Joseph and Charlie Clore are not brewers either. They are property tycoons. That is the way they look at your pubs, as property investments.'

delegate to a meeting of the Watney Mann Tenants Association, held in East London.

In 1959, Charles Clore bid £21M in an attempted takeover of Watneys. Although this bid caused an unprecedented panic in the beerage, it proved unsuccessful. In 1972, Maxwell Joseph tried again where Charles Clore had failed. On March 10 Grand Metropolitan Hotels announced a £350M bid for Watneys. In the months that followed, this bid was raised and raised again; the Rank Organisation entered and left the bidding; Watneys workers supported their board's resistance, but the tenants didn't; the odds quoted by Ladbrokes on the outcome of the bid swung one way and then the other; and the public was entertained by a slanging match between the directors of both companies. One hundred and fifteen days after the original bid was made, Maxwell Joseph was able to declare that he had gained control of Watneys. The price had risen to £420M during the bidding, exactly twenty times the price that Charles Clore had offered thirteen years beforehand. Both of these bids have had a profound effect on the brewing industry, and the difference in size between them indicates the rapid growth of the brewing giants during the 1960s.

The activities of Watneys management prior to Maxwell Joseph's bid are interesting. Watney shares had been climbing for some months in response to rumours that a takeover attempt was about to be launched. In an effort to protect their company, Watneys management bid successfully for two companies in the first quarter of 1972. International Distillers and Vintners was taken over, and Samuel Webster, a Halifax brewery with 268 pubs in the West Riding, was also swallowed up. The logic behind the takeover of Samuel Websters is not immediately apparent. Only six months previously, Watneys had announced plans to increase the capacity of their Newton Heath, Manchester, brewery by 40%, so that it would be able to supply all their outlets in the north of England, and many in the Midlands as well. It is quite clear then, that it was not Webster's brewery that Watneys wanted, but the pubs.

The spate of primitive takeover grabs which has re-shaped the brewing industry in the last ten years, has been prompted by two motives. Charles Clore's 1959 bid for Watneys was intended to take advantage of the situation in which that company's pubs and off-licences represented an under-valued and under-exploited asset. Where such a situation exists, and taking into consideration the fact that 'tied estate' accounts for over 65% of the brewing industry's assets, the scope for rationalisation, re-development and asset stripping can be very wide indeed. The discovery of this principle caused dog to devour dog with both speed and relish throughout the 1960s. In the last four years, the stock market has at least ensured that juicy takeover morsels are no longer so cheap to come by. It seemed that the boom in bids and mergers within the brewing industry was ending: the smaller brewers had become too expensive for the giants, and the giants had not been threatened from outside the industry since Charles Clore was successfully resisted in 1959.

59

But in 1968 Unilever attempted to merge with Allied Breweries. Grand Metropolitan Hotels won Trumans in 1971, and then Watneys a year later. Imperial Tobacco followed up with a successful bid for Courage. A new motive was created to reinforce the process by which the giant brewery companies were eliminating their smaller brethren. Watneys quite clearly paid over the odds for Samuel Webster, and didn't even need the extra production capacity. The Watneys bid for Websters represented an attempt to grow beyond the clutches of an even larger and more powerful giant.

The events of 1959 and 1972 provide the key to the period that falls between them, in which the face of the British brewing industry was changed out of all recognition.

In 1960 there was no such thing as a national brewery in the style of Allied Breweries or Bass Charrington, for example. A handful of prestige beers, Bass, Worthington, Guinness, were distributed nationally, but through the free trade rather than through their companies' own pubs. (Even today, Guinness owns no pubs in the U.K., relying entirely on free trade outlets.) It is interesting to compare the approximate number of pubs owned in 1960 by the nucleus companies that have spawned the big six giants, with the number of pubs those giants own today.

	1960		*1972*
Ind Coope	2500	Allied	8000
Charrington	2400	Bass Charrington	9300
Courage	3500	Courage	6000
Scottish & Newcastle	1700	Scottish & Newcastle	1700
Watneys	4000	Watneys	6000
Whitbread	2500	Whitbread	8500
	16600		39500

These companies now control 56.0% of all pubs, as against 24·0% in 1960, and the percentage is still rising.

Methods of growth have varied. Allied Breweries was formed in 1961 by the merger of Ind Coope, Ansells, and Tetley Walker. The principal trading areas of the three companies were in the south-east, the midlands, and the north, respectively. This merger was the first major reaction to the abortive bids of Charles Clore for Watneys and of Eddie Taylor (Canadian chief of Carling) for a number of English breweries. Allied has since maintained the status it achieved in 1961 of being the largest drinks group in Europe mainly by the takeover of companies with associated interests, such as Showerings which was obtained in 1968.

Both Bass and Charrington, who merged in 1967, had already been involved in vigorous takeover activities. Charrington gained control of United Breweries in the early 1960s, and Bass was taken over by Mitchells and Butlers at about the same time. Within a year of M and Bs conquest of Bass, half the latter's management had been fired or had resigned. And within a year of the final Bass Charrington merger, no less than five breweries owned by the new group had been closed. This is being followed by a further seven in the north west and south Wales, when the company's Runcorn brewery is fully operational.

Courage achieved a national chain of outlets later than its competitors. Although Georges of Bristol and Holes of Newark were taken over in the early 1960s, the group was heavily reliant on its trade in the south-east until John Smiths of Tadcaster (2000 pubs) and Plymouth Breweries (250 pubs) were acquired within three months of each other at the turn of 1970 and 1971. Courage's have not yet published their anticipated programme of brewery closures. Watneys, in contrast, announced in 1971 that they planned to shut four major breweries at Brighton, Northampton, Trowbridge and Whitechapel. All were

obtained as a result of takeovers in the 50s and 60s. Scottish and Newcastle alone among the big six has not been involved in the takeover rush, the 'primitive grab for outlets', preferring the course of extending its business through the free trade, particularly in parts of England where it was poorly represented ten years ago.

Whitbread has pursued the most unusual, and ultimately the most devastating course of expansion. As early as 1950, smaller brewers were gathered under the Whitbread 'umbrella'. The deal was usually something like this: Whitbread would take a stake in the smaller brewer's equity, would place two directors on the board, who provided advice on financial and technical problems. Whitbread was supposed to provide security from take-over attacks from other sources. In return, Whitbread products were distributed in the smaller brewer's pubs, and in this way the parent company's free trade was substantially increased. These arrangements did not begin to go sour until Whitbread's competitors chose more direct means of expansion. Then like for like was returned with a vengeance. During the 1960s, Whitbread took over twenty-one brewery companies, and fifteen breweries were shut, facts which do not square well with the bene-volent image which the company's President, Colonel W. H. Whitbread likes to project. There are indications too, that the Colonel's regiment has not finished taking prisoners. Graham Turner, the economist, has written of the remaining 'associated' companies that 'Whitbread clearly intends to mop up the rest at an appropriate moment.'*

The closure of the smaller breweries that the big six have taken over has been accompanied by the construction of enormous new plants to replace them. Reference has already been made to Bass Charrington's Runcorn develop-

*Business in Britain, Graham Turner, Pelican 1971.

ment. Allied has spent £12M on extending its Burton-on-Trent brewery, which produces Double Diamond, probably the country's top-selling keg beer, and certainly the most heavily advertised. Whitbread has opened two new breweries at Luton and Samlesbury (between Blackburn and Preston), at an estimated cost of £7M each. There are many other instances of such developments on a slightly lesser scale, and at slightly lower costs. The rationale behind these new breweries is, of course, that they make beer cheaper to produce, although it is noticeable that the new brands are usually more expensive for the customer to buy. One of the major cost savings apart from labour is in excise duty. The excise authority allows for 6% wastage in its assessment of the brewers' liability, which is geared partly to volume. The actual wastage in the new breweries can be brought as low as 2%. In other words as much as 4% of production in a modern brewery can be duty free. The customer, of course, continues to pay his $5\frac{1}{2}$ pence duty on each pint, which goes straight through into brewery profits, on top of savings made by reductions in original gravity. The only justification for these new breweries is the improvement in efficiency they make possible. It is clear, though, that these improvements do not benefit the beer drinker, who as well as receiving a more insipid pint, usually has to pay more for it. The improvements in efficiency do not seem to benefit employees either. Brewery closures and the consequent redundancies have added thousands of names to the unemployment register in dozens of towns. The key to where the benefits go lies in a study of the profits the brewing giants are turning in.

The most recent comparable figures available show the following pre-tax profits for the big six:

Allied—year ending September 1972 £53·6M (previous year £41·5M)
Bass Charrington—year ending September 1972 £48·9M (previous year £38·3M)

Courage—year ending January 1972 £14·8M (previous year
£12·1M)
Scottish & Newcastle—year ending April 1972 £20·4M
(previous year £17·2M)
Watneys—year ending September 1972 £29·8M (previous year
£16·6M)
Whitbread year ending April 1972 £20·9M (previous year
£15·9M)

The average increase from one year to the next is 33%, a
figure well in advance of inflation. A more revealing
comparison perhaps, is provided by considering the profits
of these companies in the early 1960s. In its first year of
operation, Allied made just over £6M. Comparable figures
are: Charrington £1½M, Courage £2½M, Scottish and Newcastle and Whitbread, £3M each, and Watneys £4M. In
view of these burgeoning profits it is difficult to understand how the brewers can justify their continually rising
prices, a trend which remained more active than most
until the government's freeze was imposed in the final
quarter of 1972. It is not even as if the accruing profits
were desperately required for capital projects. On the
evidence of recent spending by the big six, this cannot be
the case. In 1968, the giants, including Guinness, gave
away £100,000 for political purposes. Watneys alone spend
not far short of that on football sponsorship every year, for
the Watney Cup and its Scottish equivalent, the Drybrough
Cup. (These competitions, incidentally, are considered to
be a joke by most players and spectators, and are an
embarrassment to the football authorities because of the
way they add to the fixture jam).

The process by which Allied Breweries, for example,
have increased profits from £6M in 1961 to £49M in 1972
is not simply selling more beer more profitably. As well as
breweries, wine merchants, off-licence chains, distilleries,
hotel groups, soft drink companies, have also been taken
over. The extent to which all types of drink are manu-

factured and distributed under the banner of the big six breweries is not widely known, because subsidiaries are usually allowed to continue trading in their own names. But the trend is a powerful one, and with the advent of Maxwell Joseph, who controls Express Dairies as well as Watneys and Truman, it could be said that a milkman has bought a couple of breweries in order to get in on the wines and spirits market. The following chart lists only the major domestic subsidiaries of the big six. Most of them are household names. A quick glance will show how, for example, these brewers are responsible for more than 60% of wines imported into this country:

Allied Breweries:	Grants of St. James (vintners)
	Showerings (Babycham etc.)
	Ind Coope Hotels
	Britvic (soft drinks)
	Coates, Gaymers and Whiteways (cider)
	Harveys of Bristol (sherry)
	Victoria Wines (off-licences)
	Curtis Distillery
	Glen Rossie Distillery
	Minster (soft drinks)
	Trust Houses Forte (25% holding)
	Skol International (lager—31% holding)
Bass Charrington:	Hedges and Butler (vintners and off licences)
	Crest Hotels
	Canada Dry (U.K.) (soft drinks)
	Old Bushmill's Distillery
	Carling (lager—long term franchise from Canadian Breweries)
	Taunton Cider (27·5% holding)

Courage:	Saccone and Speed (vintners)
	Charles Kinloch (vintners)
	W. H. Thackwray (soft drinks)
	Arthur Cooper (off licences)
	Acorn Hotels
	Anchor Hotels and Taverns
	Harp Lager ($33 \cdot 3\%$ holding)
	Cantrell & Cochrane (soft drinks $29 \cdot 0\%$ holding)
	Taunton Cider ($40 \cdot 9\%$ holding)
Scottish and Newcastle:	Mackinlay-Mcpherson (wines and spirits)
	Glenallochie Distillery
	Isle of Jura Distillery ($73 \cdot 0\%$ holding)
	Harp Lager ($33 \cdot 3\%$ holding)
Watneys:	Westminster Wine (off licences)
	International Distillers and Vintners
	Coca Cola Southern Bottlers
	Peter Dominic (off licences)
	Carlsberg (U.K.) (49% holding)
	Cantrell & Cochrane (soft drinks $31 \cdot 3\%$ holding)
	Taunton Cider ($19 \cdot 5\%$ holding)
Whitbread:	Stowells of Chelsea (vintners)
	Heineken Ltd (lager)
	R. White & Sons (soft drinks)
	Threshers (off licences)
	Rawlings (soft drinks)
	Whitly Inns (hotel development jointly with J. Lyons)

It would be foolish, of course, to suggest that there is anything improper or clandestine in the way that these extensive portfolios have been accumulated. On the other hand, it certainly seems that this process has been allowed to continue far enough, and that whoever benefits from a further contentration of interests, it will not be the drink-buying public. Unfortunately, the process does not appear to have worked itself out yet. In the brewery field alone, further takeovers and mergers are certainly to be expected. It is difficult to ascertain at any given time which of the giants have what sort of stake in how many of the smaller breweries. An excellent study of this situation, however, was published by the *Financial Times* in December 1970. As a specific study, it is no longer up to date as blocks of shares have been both bought and sold since then, and some of the companies listed have actually been taken over. Nevertheless, the chart provides a general illustration of the way in which the big six are always poised to bid when an appropriate opportunity occurs. At the time of the *Financial Times* survey, Allied held a stake of more than 10% of the equity in three smaller brewers. Courage had one such holding, Watneys two, Whitbread seven and Bass Charrington ten. The number of pubs owned by the companies which seemed to be vulnerable was more than 11,000. In the intervening two years since this report was published, 4000 of these pubs have in fact fallen into the hands of the giants.

As we have seen, the giants have increased the proportion of all pubs that they own from 24% in 1960 to 56% in 1972. They are poised to go even further. The element of competition has already sunk to a dangerously low level. If current trends continue, there will soon be no alternative or contrast to the inferior produce and high-handed policies of the big six.

The adulteration of beer has already been investigated in earlier chapters, but two recent incidents will serve to illustrate the high-handedness of the giants. Firstly, after retail price maintenance was abolished, supermarkets and off-licences reduced the price of spirits. But the tenants of many breweries were forced to continue buying their supplies of spirits along with their beer. In many cases, and for many years, the brewers' wholesale prices were in excess of the supermarkets' retail prices. When Bass Charrington discovered that nine of their tenants in Yorkshire had bought where spirits were cheapest, these men were given notice to quit. Secondly, when Watneys' so-called revolution changed Red Barrel into Red in 1971, apart from the enormous cost of advertising, and the research involved in giving a so-called premium bitter a sweeter taste, the cost of changing over the cowls on bar counters exceeded £100,000. Ultimately, it is the customer who pays for these frivolities. Watneys claimed they were reacting to a shift in demand at the time of the Red Revolution. Did they seriously believe that, given a free choice between a penny off a pint or a new set of lurid lights, the beer drinker would opt for the latter?

These are no more than catchy examples that demonstrate an attitude. But it is this attitude that is wreaking havoc in the English pub, and has caused over half a million people to brew their own beer, and to drink it at home. It is this attitude that has led many brewers to throw hundreds of their tenants out on the street for the crime of building up successful businesses; that has led them to gut some of their finest pubs on the advice of market research men and accountants who are more interested in fashion and a fast buck than the tradition of centuries; that has led them to shut down hundreds of country pubs leaving villagers with nowhere to go for a drink. These are some of the issues we shall be investigating in subsequent chapters.

HENLEY

MINERA

MANUF

REWERY.

WATER

CTORY.

5. The Independent brewers

'We don't need to be taken over, we brew jolly good beer already.'

EWART BODDINGTON, of Boddington's Brewery, Manchester, explains the reason for his company's resistance to Allied Breweries' takeover bid in 1970.

'The future of quality products in the British brewing industry depends almost entirely on the continued independence of the surviving small breweries. Unless the giants have to face genuine competition from the smaller firms, we shall be forced to drink what we are told to like, or otherwise to go dry.'

What's Brewing, Journal of CAMRA, the Campaign For Real Ale.

The big six brewers own slightly less than 60% of the country's pubs, and account for slightly more than 70% of our total beer output. There are very few corners left in these mighty empires where the old recipe for a successful pub—a good pint at a fair price, served in a friendly manner in comfortable but not oppressive surroundings— remains intact. The occasional pubs belonging to the major groups that have survived so far are difficult for the public to seek out, but much easier for the brewers to weed out and add to the growing stack of chrome and plastic. It is clearly not in the interests of the big six to allow a genuine variety and competition within the houses of their groups. Worse still, the competition that exists between the groups lies more in the realms of disputed takeover bids and escalating television advertising than in any real effort to produce a better, more fairly priced product.

Two thirds of the brewing companies operating in 1960 have since been wiped out. The third that remains includes

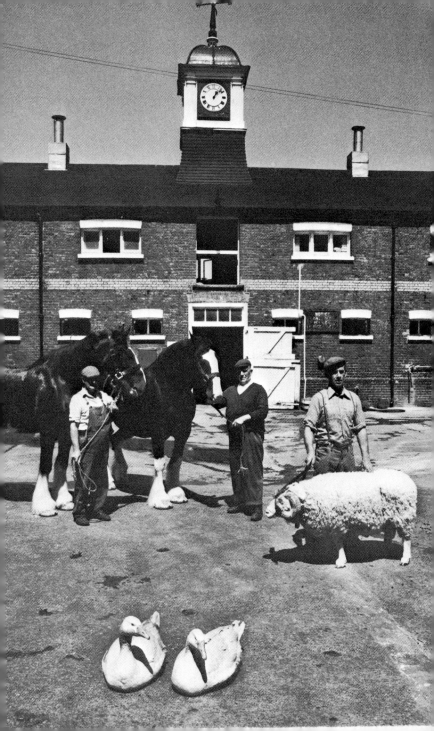

about ninety independent companies, although scarcely a month passes in which this number is not further reduced. Sadly, many of the remaining independents have aped the activities of the big six, largely because of inept managements which hold the misplaced view that this is the best way to survive. In fact, the most successful independent brewers tend to be those who have kept faith both with their customers and their better traditions. They are now beginning to fill the massive gap between real and induced demand that has been created by the demolition gang tactics of the big six.

Youngs of Wandsworth is one of the two remaining independent brewers in London. Youngs has survived the post-war decimation of London breweries by applying up-to-date management skills to the simple philosophy of providing traditional beer in traditional pubs. The company's 135 houses, mostly in South London, offer a genuine alternative to the vast majority of the pubs with which they compete. It is proving to be an increasingly popular alternative. There is a Youngs pub less than half a mile from where I write, and I know that if I don't arrive by half past eight in the evening I won't get a seat, and if I'm not there by nine it will be difficult even to get in. The company's chairman, John Young explains:

'We've stuck our necks out, and now we're in the position of the bakers who make real bread and have lengthy queues outside their shops.'

Although Youngs is a public company, the family retains a majority shareholding and John Young is the great-great-grandson of the founder. The company has a remarkable tradition of family loyalty among its staff—one man in the brewing room is a sixth generation Youngs worker. This loyalty has probably developed as a result of the strand of benevolent paternalism that runs through the company's history. The modern interpretation of this

78

theme has led to the institution of a profit-sharing scheme and the employment of a company doctor for fewer than two hundred staff.

Youngs passed through something of a crisis in the mid-fifties when the chairman died and other members of the Young family withdrew from the day-to-day running of the business. It was at this time that John Young entered the firm, and he has been its chairman since 1962. He is a firm supporter of traditional methods, and of playing fair with his customers. No substitute materials are used at Youngs brewery. The company's ordinary bitter has a hop bitterness and aroma that is rare nowadays, and the special bitter is one of the strongest pints in the South of England. The total of 135 pubs within a narrow radius from Wandsworth means that the tenants do not feel remote from 'head office' and the company doesn't lose touch with its pubs and its customers. Youngs' tenants generally add a friendly and cheerful touch to the atmosphere of the pubs, although there are one or two exceptions. But it is rarely in a Youngs house that the customer is treated in the surly fashion that is all too common now in vast numbers of London pubs. John Young is an unusual company chairman in that he seems to be just as interested in the concept of service as that of profit. In a recent annual report, his statement read:

'It is frequently said that we should return to a fair day's wage to which I would add a pound's worth of value and service for each and every pound of the price.'

The food industry has thrown up Sainsbury's, clothing has given us Marks and Spencers, and the John Lewis Partnership prospers in the sphere of department stores. It is a shame that the big six in the brewing industry with their thousands of pubs have left it to a relatively small local brewery to demonstrate that exceptionally high standards of service and value are not incompatible with profitability.

John Young is one of the few company chairmen in the brewing industry who is prepared to comment freely on the activities of his competitors. He regrets the sequence of takeovers in which hundreds of independent companies have been 'steamrollered', and is not sanguine about the future if the trend is allowed to continue:

'If everything becomes subject to the dictates of accountants, marketing consultants, and so on, the profitability of the brewing industry may well increase. But we could find ourselves in a dreary world in ten years time—a world of consistent mediocrity, in which no one is much able to enjoy the extra money in his pocket.

'I'm already worried by the way some of our competitors are changing their pubs out of all recognition, although we tend to do quite well out of it. But in a city like London, the friendly traditional pub provides a useful defence against loneliness, and a pleasant extension of people's often inadequate homes.

'Fun pubs and trendy pubs may be all right for Leicester Square and The Kings Road, but they aren't really what the majority of Londoners want. There was a lovely old Victorian pub in West London that's just been given the treatment. Waterfalls cascade on each floor through bars, restaurants and a discotheque. You have to cross a drawbridge to get in. I've often been tempted to go to the bar on the top floor there armed with a few packets of Tide.'

Their situation in London gives Youngs advantages that many of their fellow independents do not share. Their pubs are easy for millions of people to reach and provide an alternative that is particularly well defined, because nowhere are the general trends towards gimmickry, inferior products and high prices as advanced as they are in London. These advantages certainly do not apply so powerfully to Theakstons of Masham, who are nevertheless as successful as Youngs even if on a lesser scale.

Masham (situated beyond Ripon in the dales of North Yorkshire) is a small town arranged round an enormous market square. Theakstons have only sixteen tied houses, which are spread up to a distance of forty miles from the brewery. More than twenty people work for the company, which is the largest employer in Masham. Theakstons faced serious problems in 1968 when the two elderly members of the family who had been running the firm retired simultaneously. Paul Theakston became managing director at the age of twenty-three, and now runs the business with a cousin of his own age.

Paul Theakston and David Bruce are certainly the youngest management team in the brewing industry. Like Youngs, their policies are aimed at promoting their traditional approach rather than ditching it. They have been remarkably successful to date.

Much of Theakstons reputation has been built on the quality of Old Peculiar, which makes up their draught beer range together with a bitter and a mild. Old Peculiar, a rich, dark and delightful brew, is possibly the strongest draught beer in the country. Yorkshiremen are no mugs when it comes to drinking beer, yet the local name for Old Peculiar is 'lunatic broth'. When Paul Theakston took over, only 20% of the brewery's business was in the free trade, which now accounts for more than half of Theakstons sales. Total sales are expanding at a rate of more than 10%, against the industry's average of only 2–3%. The sight of a pint of Old Peculiar parked on or behind the bar of Yorkshire's free houses is becoming more and more common. The recent employment of a sales representative for the first time since 1925 should help to sustain this momentum. Paul Theakston is convinced that his company has great potential:

'Although the big brewers are trying to lead public taste in the direction of fizzy beer, an enormous demand still exists for traditional products, which very few companies are interested in supplying. Obviously we can't run to the advertising budgets of the big boys, but we find that word of mouth has an even more powerful effect in the long run. After all, our sales are increasing at five times the industry average.'

Theakston's major weapon in the battle for survival and expansion is the fact that they brew better beer than the majority of their competitors. But can they do this and still remain profitable? Experts within the industry have been claiming for years that even without takeovers and mergers, the smaller brewers will be forced into extinction because of the increasing competitive advantage that the big six are able to achieve through their economies of scale. Paul Theakston agrees that this is a problem, but does not feel that it presents insuperable difficulties:

'It's true that we can't make the same savings on our production costs as the national brewers. But there's a sense in which we don't want to anyway—such measures are often at the expense of the quality of your beers, and this is where we must retain our advantage. Our savings come in other areas—we don't have to support a highly-paid but non-productive head office staff; our advertising and our distribution costs are less.

'Because of our size we're able to keep in constant touch with our tenants, and we can deal personally with problems that arise in the free trade. This gives us an edge in efficiency as well as good relations. And even if we can't afford to spend as much on developing our pubs, we can see that their character is retained rather than destroyed.

'We do make a good profit here, because we try to be efficient without taking any short cuts on materials. There must be something in our approach, because we know that many people drive a lot of miles just to drink a pint of our beer.'

It isn't just from Leeds or Newcastle they come either. A hotel manager in Buxton was surprised when he received a letter from the United States from a party who wanted to book the top floor of his hotel for a fortnight, on the single condition that he would serve them Old Peculiar. He'd never heard of the stuff, didn't even know it was beer. But he tracked Theakstons down, wrote a welcoming

letter to the U.S., and in the week before his guests arrived, he took a large van from Buxton to Masham, and returned with the back full of barrels, all of which were comfortably emptied by the discerning tourists.

The Northern Clubs Federation Brewery is in the heart of Newcastle, on a tiny $1\frac{1}{4}$ acre site that is covered by several million pounds worth of buildings and plant. Even if the Federation cannot claim transatlantic customers, it supplies beer to clubs as far away as St. Austell. A Cornish haulage contractor ferries the barrels on his weekly run to Newcastle. Early in 1972, nineteen clubs in Coventry decided they had had enough of the policies, products and prices of Ansells and M and B, the midlands subsidiaries of Allied Breweries and Bass Charrington. The Federation is now supplying them with beer. The country's only substantial co-operative brewery obviously has an appeal for clubs far outside its normal trading area. The Northern Clubs Federation Brewery is clearly providing a popular alternative service.

There was a desperate shortage of beer in the wake of the 1914–18 war, because of the scarcity of raw materials. The brewers diverted supplies from the clubs which bought their beer to their own tied houses. In 1919 a number of club committees in the north-east banded together to set up their own brewery. Their first venture, the purchase of a disused brewery at Alnwick for £10,000 was almost a fatal decision. A few weeks after the contract was signed, a brewery in Newcastle became vacant. It was in good working order, which Alnwick was not, and the cost was only £4,300—obviously a better business proposition. So the Federation bought the Newcastle brewery and decided to cut its losses at Alnwick, which never brewed a pint after the £10,000 purchase, but which cost severe mortgage repayments for a number of years.

The capacity of the Federation's production facilities in the early 1920s was less than 500 barrels a week. A change of site took place in 1930 to Forth Street. The brewery has remained on this site since then, although the premises have been developed and expanded on many occasions, and the capacity is now 7,500 barrels a week, and 600,000 bottles of beer as well. The excellence of the Federation's beer shows that modern brewing methods and large-scale production are not necessarily incompatible with high standards of quality.

As a co-operative organisation, the Northern Clubs Federation Brewery is owned by the clubs it supplies. Each of 900 clubs has a stake according to the barrelage it takes. The beer is supplied at a cheaper rate than other brewers charge and the Federation still makes substantial profits. These are distributed half-yearly to the clubs in the form of dividends. The total half-yearly dividend is nearing £1M. The fact that clubs in the Federation can supply their members with low-priced beer, and command such large dividends as well, provides an interesting indicator to the excessive profit levels of many commercial brewers.

88

The Federation's beer is good stuff too. It enjoys an excellent reputation in the north-east, and in open competition with other beers in the House of Commons, it commands a large share of the market among MP.s.

Leslie Hutchison, the Federation's General Secretary who has worked for the co-operative movement since leaving school, is in no doubt about the Federation's priorities:

'It's our job to give our members a product they deserve at a price they can afford. We believe that we succeed on both counts, although there's always room for improvement. We're also proud of the fact that the wages of our 400 employees are among the highest in the industry, and their working conditions are at least as good as anybody else's.'

The best example of the Federation's openness is the fact that it is the only brewery in the country that declares the gravity of all its beers. The Federation has also pressed for the introduction of legislation that would make it mandatory for all brewers to reveal the strength of their products. Leslie Hutchison explains why this is necessary:

'A brewery producing 20,000 barrels per week which chooses to reduce the gravity of its beer by one degree will increase its profits by half a million pounds in a year's trading. Unfortunately one degree is only the start and the customer soon finds himself paying more for a beer which is potentially weaker and certainly cheaper to produce.'

All kinds of clubs are members of the Federation. There are Liberal Clubs and Conservative Clubs as well as Labour Clubs. There are golf clubs as well as working men's institutes. These clubs provide the people who use them with a welcome alternative to the pubs that are owned by the national brewers. It is a significant fact that in the areas where the Federation is represented, their major competitors have been forced to keep their prices down and their quality up. It is a shame that such effective competition exists in so few areas of the country.

Southwold, on the Suffolk coast, is a genteel watering place that has changed little since the Victorian era. It's where the film units go when they want to catch the atmosphere of Yarmouth or Lowestoft in the times of Charles Dickens. Southwold has enjoyed a reputation for excellent beer that goes back beyond this period. Writing in 1835, a local historian said of the town's beer that it was 'universally admired for the purity and delicious flavour imparted to it not less by the unadulterated genuineness of its composition than by the intrinsic purity of the water which enters it.'

Southwold still supplies most of its own beer. Adnams Sole Bay Brewery is situated just behind the lighthouse, a couple of hundred yards from the sea-front. Adnams beers are still brewed by traditional methods and enjoy a high reputation in the company's 75 tied houses. The Brewery's chairman, John Adnams, believes that traditional beers are what his customers want:

'Our beers are not pasteurised. They are conditioned naturally in both cask and bottle. Beer has much more flavour this way. Quite honestly, some of these modern keg beers have got no ruddy taste at all.

'Mind you, I think we're lucky to be in East Suffolk. Agricultural workers, who form a large percentage of our trade, are less fickle than many other drinkers. When they find a good pint, they stick to it.

'This is also a popular holiday area, of course, and we find there are a number of people who come to stay at Aldeburgh and Southwold just so that they can drink our beer.'

It is not surprising that Adnams sales are on the up and up. Their pubs are like oases in a part of East Anglia where takeovers by Watneys and Whitbreads have been followed by rationalisation programmes, which have included the substitution of 'top pressure' and keg beers for the traditional local brews.

It is not only in the flavour of their beer that Adnams differ from their competitors. Many of their pubs are in outlying areas, and have only a small trade, just like a number of Watneys houses in North Norfolk. But unlike Watneys, Adnams are reluctant to close them down, even if this means carrying a few unprofitable pubs. Adnams have shut only four houses in the last seven years, and in every case there was another pub very close by. A fifth closure was on the cards recently, but when John Adnams received a petition from the villagers who would have been affected, he felt unable to go ahead. He explains why his company, as long as it remains under his control, could not leave a village entirely without a pub:

'In this part of the world, the village pub provides a focal point for activity that nothing else can. It's a place to meet people and discuss things in a way that would cease to happen if the pub were to go. A village that loses its pub starts to die. I would never want to be responsible for administering that kind of blow.'

91

A sense of social responsibility in the brewing industry seems to come only from men whose businesses are sufficiently compact for them to know at first hand most of their tenants and some of their customers. When the big six plan to close a pub, or a number of pubs, they use words like 'redundant' and 'units' that emphasise their distance from the lives of people who are affected by their decisions. If they are allowed to add to the thousands of pubs they own already by further takeovers, this problem can only get worse. Adnams in Southwold is a good example of a brewery that supplies its local community with much more than beer.

Youngs, Theakstons, Northern Clubs and Adnams share a common advantage in giving effect to their determination to remain independent. For a variety of reasons, they cannot be taken over while they don't want to be. Theakstons is a private company, Northern Clubs a co-operative, and while Youngs and Adnams are both public companies, family interests have a majority shareholding in each case. Boddingtons of Manchester is a public company in which the Boddington family, who retain control of the running of the business, hold less than 10% of the shares. The firm is therefore considered to be fair game for the giants to bid for, and has to defend itself in the open market.

Boddingtons has 280 pubs, most of them within a short distance from the Strangeways Brewery, but the outposts reach north to Lancaster, and south into Staffordshire. Boddingtons bitter has a high reputation in the north-west, which is probably one of the most discriminating beer markets in the country. A significant proportion of drinkers in the region are not prepared to accept what they are offered without question, and the quality and variety of local beers remain higher than in other parts. Boddingtons has a policy of retaining the characteristic flavour of its products which are designed to suit the local palate, and of

92

trying to sell them at slightly cheaper prices than its competitors charge. Although the company is large enough to generate substantial funds to spend on the improvement of its pubs, it does not believe in the installation of gimmickry. 'If you need to go in for that sort of thing, then there's something wrong with your product,' says Maurice Fitzgerland, Boddingtons' company secretary.

In 1969, Allied Breweries, whose northern subsidiary Tetley Walker is well represented on Merseyside and in the West Riding, but not so well in Manchester, decided to bid for Boddingtons. Sir Derek Pritchard announced Allied's intention to bid a week or so before Christmas, but the formal offer of £3·8M was not made until January 1970. The bid, which was made up of Allied shares as well as cash, was dismissed with contempt by Ewart Boddington, joint managing director, who described it as a 'bumph exchange', and recommended his company's shareholders to turn it down. It was made clear at this stage that Boddingtons did not only intend to resist Allied on strictly commercial grounds. A letter was sent to shareholders giving 'four non-financial reasons for rejecting the Allied bid'. They included the company's responsibilities to its tenants, and to its customers 'who welcome competition' and would be sorry to lose 'a beer which the north-west likes at the right price.'

On January 30th, Allied, who had bought a stake in Boddingtons of almost 30% by this stage, upped their bid to £4·5M, an attractive offer in view of Boddingtons stock market valuation at the time. After careful consideration, Boddingtons shareholders were again advised to reject, and Geoffrey Boddington, the chairman, followed his financial reasoning with the following statement:

'You will be only too aware that present-day pressures bear heavily towards the elimination of individuality and character in many consumer goods.

'There is an inexorable progression towards the mass-

93

produced, nation-wide product of standardised quality. These pressures apply equally to the brewery industry about which it has been said that the standards of tradition set by the independent brewers tend to control the quality of the beers made by the larger groups. If this competition were to cease—if we were left with only five large groups of brewers, British beers would decline to the American standard of cold, chilled and filtered liquids. Instead of the traditional flavours which have made British beer world-famous and unique, the public would be confronted with the limited choice, Brand X, produced, under the guise of rationalisation, by accountants.'

The majority of small shareholders continued to stand firm in spite of the attractive nature of the revised Allied offer, and Boddingtons were assisted in their defence by the fact that Whitbread, who had long held a stake in Boddingtons, backed the Manchester company in an attempt to fend off a more immediate and formidable rival. On February 4th, Allied increased its bid for Boddingtons' preference shares. By this stage, the total offer represented, on paper, an over-valuation of Boddingtons, who were advised to discontinue their resistance by their merchant bankers, Hill Samuel. Boddingtons board again advised its shareholders to reject, this time in the teeth of all conventional financial wisdom. After a fortnight or so, Allied announced that it had not received sufficient acceptances to gain control of Boddingtons, the offer lapsed, and Allied's share stake has since been sold.

The steadiness of Boddingtons' small shareholders, on whose reaction this takeover bid was decided, was remarkable in the face of an attractive and immediate cash offer. These shareholders have since been rewarded by increased profits and dividends, and the fact that their shares now stand at twice the value of the highest Allied bid. The principal reason for Boddingtons' success in the last three years has been its ability to increase its sales at a faster rate than either its local or national competitors. A recent report by a firm of City stockbrokers concluded that the only reason for these dramatically increasing sales lay in Boddingtons' ability to brew an excellent local beer that north-westerners prefer to the national brands that the big six have tried to foist upon them.

During the period of the takeover attempt, Sir Derek Pritchard, Allied's chairman at the time, gave repeated assurances that Boddingtons shareholders and customers would benefit from inclusion within a larger group.

As for the shareholders, they quite clearly gave Sir Derek the thumbs down by rejecting his company's advances. But what did the customers think? They are usually the last people to have a say in situations such as this. Both during their defence, and following their success, Boddingtons received a flood of letters from angered or anguished customers. A few random extracts from these letters will show how ordinary people react to the prospect of a takeover of their local brewery, and the subsequent loss of their favourite beer:

'It would be a pity if our palate was destroyed by the mass-produced effluent masquerading as beer sold by many of the big companies.'
(From Middleton, Manchester)

'As a regular bitter drinker when Boddingtons is available, I would like to compliment you on an excellent beverage, second to none, and also on your choice of landlords who serve the public with courtesy and homeliness.'
(From Glossop, Derbyshire)

'What Manchester needs is Manchester beer for Manchester people, not Brand X beer for Admass Londoners.'
(from Sale, near Manchester)

'My observation is that these bids are very seldom beneficial to the customer. For instance, some of the brews on sale today are little more than sweetened water, and so far as keg beer is concerned, I regard it as a public fraud.'
(from Preston, Lancs)

'Please add my husband's name to your list of supporters as he will travel miles to drink your very good bitter, and swears there is no other beer to touch it.'
(from Prestwich, Manchester)

'I find it almost impossible to comprehend the logic of a situation in which the major brewery combines incur heavy production and distribution costs, recouped by premium prices, in marketing de-natured keg beers that nobody wants.'
(from Wilmslow, Cheshire)

'Congratulations! Who knows, Manchester may yet become a tourist attraction if only to enjoy a good drink of Boddingtons beer.'
(from Manchester)

'May you continue to brew your excellent ales forever.'
(from Dukinfield, Cheshire)

Not only in the quality of their beer, but also in the way they treat their tenants, react to their customers, improve their pubs, the best of the independent brewers provide an invaluable yardstick against which the deteriorating standards of the big six may be judged. Where they are powerful in relation to the size of their local market, as with Boddingtons and Northern Clubs, they can even put a brake on rising prices and declining quality. Where they are not so large or strong, as with Youngs, Theakstons and Adnams, they provide an alternative for the increasing numbers of people who are forced to seek it. Boddingtons' stand against Allied Breweries was in the best David and Goliath tradition. Boddingtons continued independence has clearly benefited the consumer. 'In the consumer's interest' is a fashionable phrase in parliament these days. Politicians of all colours flock to espouse the new cause. If their enthusiasm were for the most part anything more than mere talk, there would no longer be any need for the independent brewers to stage last ditch stands against powerful predators who so clearly threaten the public interest.

6. Notice to quit

'The way in which brewers are kicking people out of their pubs for no reason at all is becoming a scandal. It is an appalling business. Nothing has disturbed me more during the past twelve months than the way in which tenants are being told to leave because they have committed a crime against themselves—building up their business. Replaced, by managers, they are being penalised for being successful. I know of no other trade in the country where this could happen.'

GUY BRADY—Chairman, Lincensed Victuallers' Central Protection Society of London.

In 1970, Watneys became the first brewing company to pursue openly a policy of replacing their tenants by managers. The difference between the two categories of licensee is that the tenant leases his pub from the brewery and buys his supplies from them at wholesale prices, while the manager is a salaried employee of the brewery, which collects both retail and wholesale profits from sales made through managed houses. The tenant who builds up a good trade will generally make an excellent living, and it is his cut as well as their own that the brewers are after when they evict their tenants and replace them with managers.

Watneys started to give notice to tenants in the London area in the spring of 1970. The scale of this first round of evictions was not known until mid-July, when Watney tenants held meetings to discuss the situation. One by one, those affected added their names to the growing total. There was Jimmy Abrams from the White Swan, Bayswater. During his five and a half years as tenant, trade had multiplied five times. Toley Cooper, from the George at Hayes, had been a tenant since 1945. He was given notice to quit verbally and in front of his staff. Eddie O'Connor, a Watney tenant for twenty-two years, had spent the last four in the Castle at Childs Hill, where he had spent £9000 of his own money on improvements, and trebled the trade. James Dempsey was ordered to leave the Bell, Ilford, where he had been tenant for twenty-one years, and had built up a thriving trade from scratch. James Crossland, from the Hope at Brixton, a Watney tenant for nineteen years, asked the company representative who broke the news to him why he was being sacked. 'It's the march of time and part of the company's new policy,' he was told.

This new policy was not publicly announced before the sackings started. It was not even discussed with the official trade bodies representing the licensed victuallers' interests. The axe was wielded without warning of any kind. By the end of July, however, Watneys were forced to reveal the extent of the notices they were dishing out. Eighty had already been dispatched to tenants in London and the Home Counties, and they were part of a national programme that would eventually affect even greater numbers. This was undoubtedly the biggest crisis ever to hit the licensed trade, whose organised representatives, polite men used to dealing cooperatively with the brewers on the problems of individual licensees, or small groups, were unprepared and ill-equipped to face a problem of this scale. Jack Murphy, one of the Watney tenants under notice said at the time:

'The Central Board, with its eyes shut tight and hands over its ears, made for the cupboard under the stairs. The National Federation carried on with the ball, fully intending to deal with the flood after the last waltz.'

Unwilling to leave matters in the hands of these organisations, a group of those affected, led by Gerald Richardson, a young licensee in North London, formed the Watney Mann Tenants Association. The membership

102

jumped from 100 to 500 as the result of a meeting held on August 11th at which a seven-point 'irritation plan' was adopted. The National Federation was forced to react to this challenge to its leadership, and the following day issued an appeal to its members that was to have a crucial bearing on the developing situation. Against legal advice Arthur Boardman, the Federation's Secretary asked all his members in pubs other than Watney pubs, to cease stocking any Watney produce. If implemented, this ban would have dealt a sharp blow to Watneys trade. The company therefore offered to suspend all the notices until compensation details could be agreed. The right to negotiate the issue had at least been achieved.

The period of wrangling that followed ended in October, when greatly improved compensation terms for the sacked tenants were finally agreed and their period of notice was extended by up to two years. But their jobs had not been saved, and no limitation was placed on the number of tenants who would be forced to vacate their pubs in the future.

If the first round had gone to Watneys, however, the newly-formed Watney Mann Tenants Association was rapidly growing in membership, ideas and organisation. Gerald Richardson, who is still the chairman, remembers the early days of the struggle in 1970:

'There was a dictatorial attitude so deeply ingrained in brewery officialdom at the time that they wouldn't recognise us or negotiate with us at first. They seemed to think it was a damned cheek on our part to question their decision, even though our businesses and homes were at stake.

'The few of us who first got together really felt like orphans of the storm. It was so difficult to get people to join us, because tenants are naturally loath to offend the brewery, even when they're under notice. They feel it might jeopardise the compensation they get or their chances of being offered another pub.

'Our strength turned out to be the fact that Watneys had

103

deliberately picked out the best tenants who had built up the most successful houses, because these would yield most profit under management. These people had a bit of go in them—they already had the best pubs, and weren't prepared to take run-down houses and start all over again. Who wants to take a step backwards in life?'

After a lull of a year of so, Watneys again began to issue eviction notices on a wider scale than in 1970. News came filtering in to the Watney Mann Tenants Association of the individuals concerned. Lionel Gordon was sacked from the Norfolk Inn, Peterborough, after quadrupling the trade in just two and a half years. His regulars threatened to boycott the pub if he went. Herbie Spencer, from the Chequers at Barkingside, a former governor of the Licensed Victuallers School, received his notice too. A petition in the area against his dismissal was signed by thousands, which disproves the point made to me by one brewer that 'it doesn't matter a tinker's cuss to the customer whether a pub is run by a manager or a tenant'.

Herbie Spencer explained why it did matter to his customers as well as to himself and his family, who had been Watney tenants continuously for over fifty years.

'This is the last family house left in the area. In addition to a saloon and lounge, it has a large public bar, which would vanish under management. My customers don't want to lose the public bar. Apart from the price angle, it provides a base for three darts teams and two loan clubs. If the pub goes under management these will be swept away, for it's the brewery's policy not to run loan clubs under management and darts teams are not encouraged.'

From the information they were receiving, it seemed to the Watney Mann Tenants Association that the new wave of sackings was likely to affect around 600 houses. Each dismissal could be expected to have consequences for its local community similar to those at Herbie Spencer's pub. By now, the WMTA was a strong organisation and early

106

in 1972 it was dealt a further powerful card when Grand Metropolitan Hotels bid for Watneys. It was an unprecedented step when the tenants refused their support for Watneys' resistance until and unless they were given a fair deal themselves. Their publicity at the time reflected the company's own propaganda. One of their broadsheets read:

'If Watneys expect Watney tenants to keep Watneys Watneys, then they should keep Watney tenants tenants. Loyalty cuts both ways.'

In their desperate search for support, Watneys were forced to make considerable concessions to their tenants, although final agreement was not reached until August, by which time Watneys was safely within Maxwell Joseph's fold. The number of evictions in addition to the original 80 was brought down to 340, and the company agreed not to exceed this figure within the subsequent five years. The compensation achieved for those who would still go was many times more generous than the terms first offered in 1970.

Gerald Richardson sums up the achievements of the Watney Mann Tenants Association:

'We have succeeded in slowing down the trend to management, but not in halting it. We've got greatly improved compensation for the tenants affected. 75 per cent of Watney tenants are now members of this organisation, and we will be able to hold the company to the promises made in 1972.'

As with other adverse trends in the brewery industry, where Watneys have led others have followed. Early in 1973, for example, 60 of Trumans 800 tenants received notice to quit simultaneously. It isn't, of course, always necessary to give notice to get rid of a tenant. You can simply put the rent up instead, and some breweries have been doing this. Others simply wait until tenants either die or leave of their own accord, and then instal a manager.

Of the big six, only Whitbread (to their great credit in this respect), and Scottish and Newcastle (who have already a very high proportion of managers), are supporting the role of their tenants.

Charles Farrow, a tenant licensee for twenty seven years had spent most of that period at the Elephant and Castle in Kensington, a Bass Charrington pub which was run-down when he took it over in the late fifties, and which is now one of the busiest houses in the area. He is also Chairman of the Bass Charrington Tenants Association, which has had to deal with the same problem as its Watney counterpart, although on a smaller and more sporadic scale. The brewery refused to recognise the group in the first months after its formation, and the reaction of one Bass Charrington director, D. R. Ledward, demonstrates the point made by Gerald Richardson about the big brewers' dictatorial attitude. He said at a trade dinner at which Charles Farrow was present:

'We will not negotiate with a pressure group of self-appointed Don Quixotes tilting at real or imaginary windmills, even though their propaganda activities would win the admiration of the late Dr Goebbels.'

The windmills are real enough. Many Bass Charrington tenants have been sacked, and Charles Farrow has fought tirelessly on their behalf.

He holds strong views on the changes in brewery attitudes towards their tenants that have taken place in the last ten years, and on the effect these changes are having on the general public.

'Up till then I was happy to be a brewery man. I identified entirely with their policies. It was pleasant to deal with them, and there was a genuine partnership that benefited both sides as well as the public.

'There's been a complete change since then. Instead of encouraging their best tenants, they want to take their pubs away from them. There's no longer any prospect of promotion for a good young tenant in a small house, because all the bigger pubs are going under management.

'Managers are more tied to their own brewery for stocks, and have to promote the items the brewery wants to push rather than those which their customers want. Managers tend to change rapidly, where tenants stay much longer. This disturbs the staff, and spoils the atmosphere for the customers.

'The brewers tart up their managed houses with appalling and stereotyped taste, rather than let a tenant provide the atmosphere suitable for a particular pub and its trade.'

Charles Farrow described himself to me as a 'martyr as yet unburned.' He can now remove the qualifying clause; he received his notice to quit the Elephant and Castle, in my view one of London's best run pubs, in May 1973. He explains why he is the last of five generations of publicans in his family:

'My son would have made a fine publican but I am glad that I managed to persuade him to enter a different profession. There is no future for a young man in the licensed trade.'

Edward Rivers, Secretary of the Licensed Victuallers Central Protection Society of London, is greatly concerned about the effect that the brewers' managed house policies are likely to have on the quality of future entrants to the trade:

'Excellent tenants are being penalised for the very fact of their success. This disincentive, that the more successful you are, the more likely you are to be dismissed, is unique in British industry. The calibre of new tenants entering the licensed trade will be drastically reduced if this trend continues.'

Arthur Boardman, Secretary of the National Federation of Licensed Victuallers is also disturbed by the gathering trend to managed houses, on behalf of the public interest as well as that of his members:

'Management in pubs deprives the public of the initiative. When it becomes clear to a tenant what his customers want in the way of facilities and the range of drinks, it is in his own

interest to provide for these requirements. Managers are subject to the remote control of head office staffs in large brewery groups, and can be required to provide what the brewery wants the public to have.

'In the sphere of catering, for example, managed houses are often directed to the expense account end of the trade rather than to the cheap lunches laid on by a tenant's wife.

'The process is being intensified by the takeover of more and more breweries into large units that are already, in some cases, too big to operate efficiently. There are many small brewers who are more profitable on a pro rata basis than their national competitors. But they still get taken over. Efficient but small economic units are destroyed to create large but inefficient ones. The leeway is then made up by taking it out on the tenant, either by increasing his rent by a vast amount or by replacing him with a manager. The property development mentality, if generally applied, could mean the destruction of the public house as an institution.'

The numbers of managed houses continue to increase in spite of the tenants resistance, and the clear fact that the trend is not in the long-term interests of the public. In London alone, the number of managed houses has almost trebled from 400 to more than 1100 since 1959. The national percentage is also increasing, and now stands at more than 25 per cent. These 25 per cent account for more than 40 per cent of total pub trade as they are generally the bigger houses. This is also the sector of their tied estates on which the big brewers concentrate their investment. The point was well made in a newsletter circulated by a Licensed Victuallers Association in North London:

'Some brewers, especially Watneys, think nothing of lashing out £40,000 for their managed Instant Atmosphere Palace, and some so-called designers must be making fortunes.'

It should be said at this stage that individual managers are in no way the villains of the piece. A good manager

112

will run a better pub than a poor tenant. It is also true that there are a number of very large, city-centre, entertainment pubs that are perhaps better run under management than tenancy. It is the increasing encroachment on the tenanted sector of pubs that is the disturbing trend.

The effects of this trend have been damaging enough already. There are nevertheless signs that the worst has yet to come. Sheppards and Chase, a firm of stockbrokers who are keen students of the brewing industry have recently made the following forecast:

'At present just over one quarter of the public houses in the UK are managed and we believe this proportion will rise to perhaps 50 per cent by 1980 partly because most new outlets are put under managed operation and also because tenants will gradually be replaced by managers.'

If this forecast is accurate it will mean that more than 15,000 pubs will be transferred from tenancy to management in little more than six years, a process that Sheppards and Chase refer to as one of 'gradual replacement'. Thousands of tenants will lose their businesses and their homes, and all will lose their chance of progress in the licensed trade, as a reward for running a successful pub. Hundreds of thousands, possibly millions of customers, will find that their locals have come under the direct control of the breweries, who will instal managers and change the nature of the pubs as they see fit. The choice of wines, spirits and mineral waters will be severely restricted to the brewers' own brands. You will get the beer you are told to like, served in the fashion that the brewers want it to be served. Pub food will become more standardised and much more expensive. The décor and the furnishings will be decided by a designer in London rather than by the landlord and his wife. Entertainment in pubs will become the rule rather than the exception and you will have to take it or go dry. If you still go for a drink, you will pay for the entertainment whether you want to watch it or listen to it or not. Entertainment in pubs is of course fine where the majority of customers want it, as are fruit machines and juke boxes. It is not fine that they should be installed where they are not wanted. One brewery recently attempted to dismiss a widowed licensee because she refused to instal a contraceptive machine in the gents. If Sheppards and Chase are right, or nearly right, Big Brother will soon be arriving in your pub. One monopoly will be impressed on another as the brewers entrench themselves against the day when a government attempts to loosen the stranglehold of the tied-house system. When you say goodbye to your landlord as he leaves, you had better say goodbye too to the pub as you know it, like it, and would prefer it to stay if your opinion, as a mere customer, carried any sway.

7. The Blitz on the pub

'There is the pub, for instance, misguidedly got up as the inside of a galleon, a Western saloon, or, for all I know, St. George's Chapel, Windsor, or a Jumbo Jet. For my money—and I suppose that's what they're after in their hopeless, twisted way—they can send all this stage-property rubbish back to the scene store at Riverside Studios . . . There's a rule on these joints, incidentally: the fancier the fittings, the worse the beer.'

BASIL BOOTHROYD

There is a tiny pub in Norwich that nestles under the walls of the cathedral precinct. The place is much the same as it must have been centuries ago—high-backed wooden settles, stone flags, tables scarred with use and worn with scrubbing. There is no bar; each drink is drawn in the cellar and carried up a narrow flight of stairs. There are few windows, the pub is dim and cool on the sunniest of days. A recent takeover placed the house within the estate of one of the major national brewers. Someone soon decided that the pub was too dark inside, too rough and ready. As the first step in a scheme to smarten things up, an electrician and his mate were sent to instal fluorescent strip lighting in this mediaeval tavern. But the brewer's estates department had reckoned without the reaction of the landlady, tenant for thirty years, now into her seventies, renowned in the city for her ferocity when crossed. The electrician and his mate were sent packing with comments that must have disturbed the peace in the cathedral close. The character of the pub was saved, temporarily at least.*

*Owing to ill-health, the landlady has recently retired, and many alterations to this pub have since been made. It is only fair to say that in this case, the new tenant has acted with respect for the pub's atmosphere, and many original structural features have been sensitively restored.

The customers of this pub were luckier than most. Countless drinkers have seen their locals gutted or damaged in the last ten years. The character of a pub can reside partially in features that are archaic, useless or simply in the way. These are ripped out and replaced by the modern comforts the brewers are so anxious to provide, and charge for. Luxurious soft furnishings replace the wooden seats, wall-to-wall carpeting covers those worn-out old tiles, the ornate mirror and the dart-board make way for a set of tasteful hunting prints.

The brewing industry has been spending £50M per annum for the last ten years or so on the upkeep and development of its tied estate. Half of this goes on building new pubs, and half on what a Bass Charrington spokesman unashamedly described to me as 'tarting and re-vamp'.

Planning a brand new pub is probably one of the most difficult assignments an architect can face. The challenge is rarely met with the resource and imagination that can create an environment in which people drink, talk, argue, sing and laugh together happily, noisily and comfortably. Most of us have visited one or more of the 500 or so new pubs that are built each year, and we tend to find them faceless, soulless, mere lounges for drinking in. The standard design emanating from the brewers' estates department is all too familiar. It can be plonked down on any site that is reasonably square and flat, preferably with tarmac on at least three sides and a prim little wall at the front. The traditional charms of structural uniqueness and eccentricity are bulldozed as flat as the site in preparation.

Such places are as uninspiring inside as out. Summarising an extensive survey of the design of new pubs, Geoffrey Salmon wrote in the *Architects Journal*,

'. . . generally the standard of furnishings and decorations is very disappointing. For the most part, they appear to have been added as an afterthought and were by no means an intrinsic part of the design. The toughness and character of the nineteenth

116

century seems generally to have given way in these new pubs to weak "clever" schemes of decoration, lacking coherence and often using an overwhelming medley of colours or patterns of different scales which the "locals" suffer under the impression that this is "contemporary" decoration.'

Specific criticisms were levelled against the lack of exposed brickwork and sculptured concrete, traditional and modern materials felt by the survey team to have great possibilities inside the new pub. Lighting was considered to be unimaginative. The patterns of carpet, furniture and curtain materials were found to be too intricate and domestic. The overall conclusion of the survey was that most new pubs are stereotyped and unwelcoming from the outside, fussy and unfriendly within.

Some architects have claimed that no good pubs have been built in the last fifty years. This is surely too great a generalisation, and a view that is insidiously conducive to a state of despair in the architectural profession, through which architects may come to believe that it is no longer possible to design a good pub. Excellent houses can still be built, as long as certain basic principles are observed.

Trying to define the constant elements in good public house design seems to be a worthwhile exercise. People form into groups, either standing or sitting, in a crowded pub. This natural process should be gently underlined by splitting the available floor space into defined areas of varying shapes and sizes. This can be achieved either structurally, with part walls or wooden partitions projecting into the bar, or with high-backed benches and settles.

Cosiness and intimacy must not be allowed to destroy the easy and relaxed atmosphere of sociability that belongs to the best pubs. Although the customer area may be sub-divided, the bar itself should always remain the focal point. Wood is the natural material for the bar structure and the shelves behind. When this is polished and merged with a display of bottles and glasses, and the

117

whole is attractively lit, the sense of warmth and well-being is hard to resist. Trade as well as bonhomie will flourish in such conditions.

There are things to avoid, as well as things to aim for. The monotony of long unbroken expanses of wall, or ceiling, or carpet, is the enemy of atmosphere in the larger pubs of today. Bright and startling wallpaper or paint is not generally suitable, although nicotine can be a useful colouring agent in toning down the worst excesses of some of the brewers' interior designers! Rich, dark colours and heavy, interesting textiles and fabrics may not be in fashion for decorating homes or offices, but they can still make a contribution to the pubs that will be built in the 1970s.

The functional apparatus of the pub should not be despised and concealed in the overall design. The possibilities of bottles, glasses, and wooden barrels where still in use are obvious, but too rarely exploited. A more unusual illustration of this point is provided by The Snowcat, a late nineteen-fifties pub in Cambridge, owned by Greene King of Bury St. Edmunds. The cellar is placed on the first floor and beer is drawn through transparent pipes which descend from the ceiling to the bar. An attractive design feature that probably has the effect of renewing thirst among those who glance in its direction, this system also has the advantage of enabling the beer to be drawn by gravity, the best means yet invented.

Respect for these elements of good pub design must be combined with a sensitivity to local needs and habits, and an eye for detail. The Prince Albert in Lowestoft was built in 1960, and belongs to the small family concern (discussed in the previous chapter) of Adnams of Southworld. It replaced a tumbledown nineteenth-century pub on the same site, and was designed by the local firm of architects, Tayler and Green. The Prince Albert has the unusual distinction of being mentioned in the Suffolk

118

volume of Nikolaus Pevsner's *The Buildings of England* series, where it is described as 'an uncommonly excellent recent pub'. It has the equally unusual and possibly more important distinction of being frequented by all the regulars of the old pub it replaced.

One detail will show the lengths the architects went to in order to appreciate the requirements for the new pub. A corrugated iron shack had served the old house for a cellar. It was on the north side of the pub and had doors at each end providing through ventilation. Both these features were repeated in the new house, and, to their surprise but satisfaction when The Prince Albert re-opened, the regulars found that the beer was just as good as it had always been.

The Prince Albert was built on a shoestring budget. Most small brewers, even the profitable ones, suffer from a lack of ready funds for expensive capital projects. Two bars, a verandah, an off licence, a cellar, and the tenant's flat were built, fitted and largely furnished for £10,500.

The national brewers may be prepared to chuck their money about when building new houses, and to employ London rather than local architects on the occasions when they put the design process out to contract. But the planning of a successful new pub is not just a matter of big money and eminent reputations. It is a deeply disturbing fact that many of the larger brewers, and the architects they employ or hire, have strayed from first principles, and are producing cold and cheerless pubs that add little to the neighbourhoods in which they are situated. All too often this happens in new towns, suburbs and housing estates where the public is offered no alternative choice.

A design that looks like a dream on the drawing board can become a nightmare in cold fact. Companies that own thousands of houses have grown insensitive to the vital individuality of each one, and are no longer fostering this tradition in the new pubs they build. In the rarefied

119

atmosphere of their executive environment, the managers of these companies have forgotten that there are lessons to be learned from something as simple as a corrugated iron shack.

The second half of the industry's tied estate budget, a further £25M a year, is spent on modernising existing houses, on 'tarting and re-vamp'. Not all of this money is squandered on surrounding the drinker with a clutter of 'stage-property rubbish', as Basil Boothroyd puts it. Many of the country's stock of older pubs are as cold and un-friendly as the new ones thrown up each year, and funds devoted to cheering them up can be money well spent. Improved sanitation and better kitchen facilities are necessary in a vast number of houses. A certain pub is too small for the custom it attracts and an extension may be justified. Much good work is being achieved in these areas, and few people would wish to quibble with such projects. But this is not where the bulk of the budget goes. Increas-ingly it is the brewers' marketing rather than estate management departments that dictate patterns of spending on their houses.

The latest craze is the installation of corporate identity schemes. In certain parts of the country Bass Charrington have painted all their pub doors red and planted illumin-ated box signs over the top. Watney Mann are placing broad strips of pillar-box red over the doors and windows, stretching round their houses as far as the eye can see. Badly-shaped and unattractive white lettering, usually out of scale with the building is superimposed on this back-ground to pick out the name of the pub, and often replaces a hanging sign. In one Truman pub, the red and orange stripes on a green background that combine in their new insignia reach from first-floor to gutter level on the side of a three-storey building forming a permanent lurid rainbow. One colour seems to figure in all these schemes; the brewers are all red revolutionaries now, and often seem to

120

approach their pubs with the finesse of Russian tanks. Unless local planning authorities waken to this threat, and put a stop to it, each pub that belongs to the major brewers will become just as much a branch of head office in appearance as a Tesco supermarket or the local Barclays Bank.

Inside the red doors, the brewers do not rest until each pub has its own theme or gimmick. Nowhere is this trend as widespread as in London, where one of the two remaining local brewers, preferring a more traditional approach, have sensed that this is what their customers want too. Youngs of Wandsworth believe that the retention of real character in their pubs is one of the factors that has led to a marked increase in trade in recent years. The case against gimmickry was eloquently made by John Young, the company's chairman, in his 1971 report to the shareholders:

' "Pubby" pubs is what we at Young's shall strive to preserve, confident that they will long outlive the gimmicky pubs which invade town life today. The current mania on the part of some brewers to gut their premises and concoct a stage set, be it a Mississippi show boat, the inside of a bus, tram or smuggler's cave, has become so frenzied that decorators don't seem to be able to ruin pubs fast enough. I see a danger that one of our greatest heritages may be spoiled or disappear through the onslaught of gimmickry, just as many of our traditional beers have disappeared.'

Egon Ronay was forced to the same conclusion early in 1972 when announcing the results of a 'pub of the year' competition conducted by his team of inspectors: 'there are pubs of great traditional character swamped by gimmickry,' he said.

The gimmick pub is a sham. It is heir to the 'Brewers' Tudor' pub of the inter-war period, a pathetic and badly-executed imitation. It is the creation of men who chant the slogan that brewing is now part of the leisure industry, and who believe that they must offer their customers the

122

excitement of the bingo hall and the bowling alley. The pub as a place to relax with good beer and good company, in surroundings that are pleasant but not oppressive, is an ideal that is betrayed by the onslaught of gimmickry.

Our younger designers have apparently decided that we need a change. Roy Wilson-Smith is the designer of some thirty London pubs for Watney Mann. In an interview published by the London *Evening Standard*, he was asked to explain his philosophy:

'I want to give people who use my houses a rare and primitive relationship with the raw forces of nature. People love to be awed when they enter a pub by a superior natural force—a strange sort of higher masochism.'

I must confess that I don't know who these people are. They are certainly not the people I have met in pubs up and down the country, who seem on the whole to prefer refreshment to punishment. But this kind of design mentality, light years removed from the atmosphere of any public bar, has the upper hand.

Thousands of pubs a year receive the treatment, in full or in part. I had visited several gimmick houses in order to produce some instances to illustrate the more general points already made. It was about this time that I came across the August 1970 edition of *Red Barrel*, Watneys house magazine. Reading the section which deals with 'improvements' to the company's tied estate, I found that *Red Barrel*'s editorial staff were illustrating the case against gimmicky pubs far better than I could hope to do. This is what they wrote about five of their pubs:

'The bar names—the Cloisters, Jolly Friar and Merry Monk— reflect the general theme of the house, which is derived from nearby Barking Abbey, a well-known ancient monument.'— The Westbury, Barking.

'A false ceiling, new bar and back counter, carpeting and new furnishings have been installed, the general decor and pictures

124

conjuring up Derby Day of years gone by.'—Derby Arms, East Sheen.

'Designed on a "cave" scheme, with imitation stalactites and stalagmites, and a bar called the "Cave Dwellers".'—The Sutton Arms, Southend.

'Previously known as "The George IV", this rebuilt house is now decorated on the theme of the honeycomb, even the cash register being hidden inside an imitation wooden hive!'—The Honeycomb, Hounslow.

'The building is octagonal and the interior decor represents the fairground, with two bars titled "Fun of the Fair" and "Swings and Roundabouts". Dominating the house in the centre is a miniature carousel, complete with horses, which revolves at a leisurely 2 rpm.'—The Carousel, Letchworth.

This represents one brewer's contribution for one month to the gimmick movement. And these are only the places that got the full works.

Pubs such as these have a limited lifetime. The trade that is attracted by the gimmicks will just as soon become bored by them, and look elsewhere for stimulation. So re-vamp follows re-vamp in a vicious circle of increasing intensity. The builders and decorators have scarcely been paid for one job when they are called in for the next. In 1970, Watneys spent £45,000 on converting the Cross Keys at Edmonton, North London, into a discotheque. Early in 1972, a further £7,000 was spent on re-styling the discotheque into an old time music hall. Bass Charrington are perhaps the biggest spenders of them all in this department. Their old-fashioned White Hart was transformed into the Chelsea Drugstore at a cost of £180,000 in 1968. By 1972 the experiment had not been a great success, and parts of the pub were converted once more to the traditional atmosphere that had been there in the first place. Bass Charrington have refused to reveal the cost of the second conversion. The reason for their embarrassment is not hard to find. It may be the brewers who sign the cheques to cover the cost of these schemes, but it's the customer who pays in the end through the increased price of his pint.

The installation of gimmickry is not the brewer's only method of forcing prices up and pushing the regulars out. It has also been decided on our behalf that entertainment is the order of the day. Entertainment in pubs, whether formal or informal, professional or amateur, is of course very much a live tradition. Music, drag, comic turns, striptease, all have their devotees and a rightful place in the pubs whose raison d'etre is entertainment. It is when a family house is turned overnight into a discotheque against the will of its regular customers, that there is cause for alarm. This is precisely what happened to the Green Gate in Ilford, the Green Man in Leytonstone, and the nine other East End pubs run by Wheatley Taverns. This company is jointly owned by Bass Charrington and Bob Wheatley, and specialises in the creation of 'fun' pubs, with pop music and go-go dancers, flashing lights, close-circuit television, and so on. The price of beer touches five bob a pint!

There is little that the regular customers can do when powerful brewers and their tenants combine to change the character of a local pub out of all recognition. Sometimes they put up with the new regime, even though they don't like it; sometimes they will be able to beat a retreat to another suitable pub in the district; or if this alternative is not available, they might just simply stay at home. It is this collective weakness of the country's drinking men and women who can be thrown out of their locals by men who know that there will be no serious consequences to face that has enabled the brewers to go the way of their own choosing, regardless of the outrage and sometimes the misery they cause. It has enabled them, for example, to make a quiet and selective start to what

126

could become their next magician's master stroke in the art of making tradition vanish, the disappearance of the public bar.

Beer is one of the most sensitive items in the cost of living index. During the currency of their prices and incomes policy, the last government pegged public bar prices for a period of three years. Many of the brewers responded by doing away with their public bars. Sometimes a partition came down and the entire pub was transformed into one enormous bar, where lounge or saloon prices prevailed. Alternatively the public was re-fitted, re-named the 'Village Bar' and price restraint was again evaded.

As the structure of society has changed since the last war, so have trends and habits in relation to the pub. A greater proportion of middle-class people are regular pub-goers than used to be the case. Women and young people represent two enormous markets that the brewers have only begun to exploit on any scale in the last fifteen years. These new customers have more expensive tastes and more money to satisfy them than the working man whose pint of mild or bitter was the brewer's basic support for decades. Their presence in the pub makes the brewers more anxious than ever to knock down the partitions and encourage the public bar trade to follow this new example.

It can be claimed that social change has made all kinds of people more willing to mix freely with one another in leisure situations. This may well be true in many pubs, but it is not a sufficient justification for the removal of the public bar. There will always be pensioners, students, working men in working clothes, who for one reason or another prefer to buy their drinks at a slightly cheaper price in slightly simpler surroundings. Such people are increasingly being deprived of their traditional alternative in this respect, and in some areas will soon find it hard to locate a pub where their custom is welcome.

In 1970, John Dickson, a Whitbread executive, gave a speech in Durham to the local Licensed Victuallers' Association. Among the points he made was this:

'It is high time that Andy Capp was given a new suit and a car and took his wife out to one of the many popular north east pubs where he can still enjoy his pint of beer and Florrie can have a glass of sauterne with her scampi and chips.'

Although cloaked in paternalism, the message to the working man is clear— smarten yourself up, bring your wife along. Ply her with wine at four bob a glass, buy her a meal at £1 a throw, and we'll be glad to serve you a pint of bitter!

The pubs that belong to the national brewers are becoming as neutral, as sterile, as the beer they serve. Stephen Gardiner, the *Observer's* architectural correspondent, captured the troubled spirit of the threatened pub in a piece he wrote for the *London Magazine* in 1966:

'What's happened to the pub, that most personal piece of English belongings? The place where you stand up and drink, where there are scrubbed oak benches to sit on, partitions to conceal private conversations, men with pipes and caps, and there is sawdust and beer on wooden floors? What's happened to those powerful bar tops, the glass flaps over the counter and the bottle-crammed shelves; the complicated cut-glass that fortified you from the fog and snow, and through which the indecipherable interior form of figures, furniture and lights made impossible shapes from the wet streets outside? What's happened—they're going, or gone, most of them. The great brewers —Watneys, Whitbreads and so on—are disposing of all that rubbish: that's out now, finished with, they say. That's dead wood, old hat. We're living in a Modern Age. Dickens is dead, you know. Did you know that? Well, some people don't. Anyone would think Victoria was still alive! Good God—there are new materials now. Chromium plate, plastic (marvellous stuff, formica—doesn't burn), wonderful new lacquers you can see your face in and, of course, artificial flowers. Last forever.

128

Well you can't beat that, can you?—Flowers that last forever. The Germans have patented an artificial scent—you just spray it on, each morning—Rose, Gardenia—have to watch you don't get your sprays mixed up, of course—not that anyone would notice. No, we don't like bare boards, these days. We have to cater for the young. Yes, yes, I know what you mean but we don't encourage *that* sort of customer any more—they've got their own pubs to go to—this place has changed hands, the street's "turned over" and that's all there is to it, we're afraid. Drinking's a business now, not a hobby. It's double gins not pints of beer we're after. Why doesn't someone introduce the treble gin?—it'll come sir, it'll come—amazing how much money there is about—even in the Freeze—just flowing like gin. Yes, we like the place to look friendly—plenty of flowers (*and* leaves, they make a rather nice dark green variety), and I like pink net formica myself although Market Research generally settles matters of taste. Close carpeting is best, so warm— avocado, salmon, peach and shrimp are popular colours. And naturally, as you see sir, we do food now . . . . A little Italian prosciuto? broad beans? a spot of corn? tomatoes?—they're lovely today, really beautiful. French bread? No? . . . . No, I'm afraid the crabs are just part of the décor. They're wax.'

The pub that millions know and love is being wrecked, deliberately, wilfully. The brewers are the vandals. The only real difference between them and the people who paint slogans on walls or tear up flowers in the park, is that the brewers will not be in court on Monday morning to answer for their actions.

8. The Dry villages

'A village that loses its pub starts to die.'

JOHN ADNAMS—Chairman, Adnams Brewery, Southwold.

The White Horse has stood in Sutton High Street for over two centuries. But Sutton, a village with a population of 200 situated near Petworth in Sussex, almost lost its pub in 1972. Allied Breweries, the owners, decided that the White Horse had become uneconomic. In spite of a petition from the villagers, and the intervention of Sir Desmond Ackner, a High Court judge who lives in Sutton, the pub was put up for auction in a Chichester saleroom. The highest bid, £26,500, was made by Ian Anstruther, the author, who felt that the pub should be kept open for the benefit of the village. He explained at the time:

'I have spent the money in defence of a principle—that villages like this should not be allowed to die. It is a lot of money. But are we to be greedy and simply get the most profit we can out of having money? Or are we to spend it for the general benefit? Sutton was becoming like a lot of other villages in the area—just a street of houses. If the pub had gone, it would have been a complete end to village life.'

Sutton was fortunate. Not every village has an enlightened fairy godfather who can afford to intervene when the brewers have decided to shut the local.

The wholesale closure of village pubs began in Norfolk in the late 1960s, after Watneys had gained control of most of the breweries and pubs in the county. In 1970 the London *Evening Standard* printed the following item:

'The Watney Mann brewing giant is finding that there are more ways to make money from a pub than by just selling beer. Up in East Anglia, the group is closing them down by the dozen. Chairman Michael Webster seems keen on the idea of selling off the less profitable houses and putting the cash to more useful purposes.'

To the chairman of a large public company, and the accountants who advise him, vast sums of money spent on football sponsorship, advertising, political donations, and so on, may well seem to serve a more useful purpose than providing beer for thirsty villagers. The people in Norfolk, however, take a different view. The widespread sense of loss felt throughout the county was identified by an excellent report filed to the *Daily Telegraph* by Simon Dring in 1970:

'Mr Orrice Bambridge, 72, who has drunk a daily pint of beer in his village's one pub since he was sixteen, now has to go to bed early with a cup of cocoa. The pub, at Barney, Norfolk, was closed last week. A few miles away, two other villages have just lost their last pub. At nearby Guist, Miss Jessie Bunn, 80, a spinster who has run her own pub single-handed for 55 years, was only saved from losing her home and livelihood by a public protest campaign.

'Dozens of village pubs have been shut in recent years and sold for conversion. Dozens more are being threatened with it in the near future. Some villages have a second pub to fall back on, but most are left beerless. Nearly all the closures have been made by Watney Mann (East Anglia) which owns most of the pubs in Norfolk. The brewery says the closures are "to maintain and subsequently improve our service".

'Mr R. L. Canham, Watney's regional trade director, says: "Norfolk has been overpubbed for many years." Rationalisation was necessary. The national average of drinkers per pub is 700. In Norfolk it is 500–600, often dropping to as low as 350. "Not enough for a profitable pub," the brewery says.

'Watneys policy of rationalisation has been strongly attacked by local councils, magistrates, and in the press. Critics also say

that redecoration, modernisation and the installation of managers instead of licensees has ruined the atmosphere and character of many pubs and caused trade to drop.

' "The locals don't want fancy paper and juke boxes," says a councillor from Fakenham, whose most popular pub has been de-popularised by garish wallpaper. "They don't want managers who talk with a London accent either."

'Major D. J. W. Sayer, a local magistrate, believes the worst aspect of the closures is that it "destroys social life" in villages, where the pub is often the only social centre.

' "The breweries seem to think everybody drives a car," says Mr A. E. Baker, the local butcher in the village of Bawdeswell (population 500), where the last pub was closed in February. "Our nearest is now four miles away. Nobody's going to walk that distance or risk a drunken driving charge by taking the car."

'At Billingford (population 200), another beerless village, old age pensioners say it will only be a matter of time before the nearest local is ten miles away. "Four nearby have been shut down in the last few months," says one.

'Watney Mann admit cases where parishes have lost their only pub "but normally there's one within two or three miles. We feel the great public benefit (from improving others) far out-weigh what we are sure is no more than occasional slight inconvenience." '

' "Considerable research, economics and the needs of the community has guided the choice of closures," says Mr Canham. But he refuses to displose the number of what he calls "con-siderable closures."

'Rationalisation is spreading to Lincolnshire and Suffolk, where advertisements announcing pubs for sale appear regularly each week.'

Indeed, it has since spread to most parts of the country where other brewers have got the message and are busy making once-and-for-all profits as they pull out of village after village. But in the case of Watneys in Norfolk, they evidently believed that they were keeping faith with the community in their actions. Phrases such as 'maintain and subsequently improve our service', 'great public benefit',

134

and 'no more than occasional slight inconvenience,' are intended seriously and the trend they describe needs to be examined closely.

Stiffkey, a village of just over 300 population, situated on the North Norfolk coast, has only ever hit the headlines once. That was in the 1930s, when the Rector was unfrocked in Norwich Cathedral and was later mauled to death by a lion he failed to tame at a Lincolnshire fairground. Since then, Stiffkey has gone quietly about its business, except for the summer months, when thousands of cars and coaches on their way to Sheringham and Cromer pour through the village, bringing trade to the general stores, but not any more to the pubs. There are no pubs left in Stiffkey, since the last was shut down in the summer of 1971. Until the mid 1960s there were three pubs in the village which had traditionally belonged to three separate breweries, each based in Norwich. All three breweries were swallowed up by Watneys, whose rationalisation programme arrived in Stiffkey when the Victoria, the former Steward and Patteson house, was closed in 1966. In 1969, it was followed by the Red Lion, which had previously belonged to Bullards, and in 1971 the pub that had once been owned by Morgans Brewery, the Townshend Arms, was shut down, put up for auction, and sold as a private dwelling.

So Stiffkey has joined the ranks of the beerless villages. In defence of these closures, Watneys explain that there are twelve alternative houses within a radius of three miles. This explanation is true in the strict sense, but nevertheless misleading, for the nearest of those twelve is almost two and a half miles from Stiffkey and most of them are in the small town of Wells-next-the-Sea, to where there are only a few dozen buses a year. Quite how the former regulars of Stiffkey's pubs, many of them elderly, are expected to travel the two and a half miles necessary in order to obtain a drink, is left unexplained by Watneys, who claim that 'no more than occasional slight inconvenience' is caused by these and other closures.

Alan Tuck, a local man who worked for the Post Office for 42 years before retiring recently, and who lives in a cottage on the edge of the village, takes a different view:

'The brewery have killed this area, they've killed off the social life of the village. People have nowhere to go now for a drink and a chat. The darts team was one of the best in North Norfolk, and there were keen cards and domino players in Stiffkey pubs. The cricket team and the football team find it difficult to get together to pick sides, and they go home straight away after matches. We can't entertain anyone any more. I wouldn't be surprised if the teams fold up completely.'

Alan Tuck is particularly bitter about the closure of the Townshend Arms, the last pub to go, a fine-looking and spacious house that commands a good position in the village. He estimates that there were as many as forty regulars, of whom half travel by car to other pubs if they want to, 'but it's not the same as your own village local,' and of whom half have no alternative but to stay at home. One of these is Dick Dowsin, an eighty year old gardener who has lived in Stiffkey all his life, and who used to enjoy going to one or other of the pubs for an hour or so each day after finishing work:

'It isn't the same village any more. I do manage to get a few bottles in at home sometimes, but that isn't much good. I mainly went for the company, to meet my friends, but I hardly see some of them at all now.'

By all account, the Townshend Arms was a thriving pub, even though it was run by an elderly couple who weren't too enterprising. Alan Tuck feels sure it was a going proposition, and could have been even more so:

'There were two good-sized bars, and a cottage on the end which they could have turned into a guest-house. There was car-parking space, and room for more—if they'd done food they

136

could have picked up a lot of the tourist trade as well as the locals. But they own nearly all the pubs round here, so they'll pick that up somewhere else anyway.'

That is probably true. Watneys will pick up the tourist trade elsewhere because they own such a heavy majority of North Norfolk's pubs. Without this near-monopoly, it is unlikely that they would have shut the Townshend Arms, and risked losing out to the competition. But shut it is, and the villagers are the poorer for having nowhere to go, while Watneys are the richer by whatever price the property fetched at auction.

Old Buckenham, also in Norfolk, is on the other side of the county, some forty miles from Stiffkey, but this distance has not saved the village from suffering a similar fate. Old Buckenham is three times the size of Stiffkey, with a population of almost one thousand, which as in many Norfolk villages is scattered over several square miles. There were three pubs in the village, catering for different parts of the community, until the Sun was closed within a month of the Townshend Arms. The Sun, situated at the Cake Street end of the village, is over a mile from either of the other pubs, and was an extremely popular house with its own band of dedicated locals, who resisted its closure with something more than the hopeless resignation that seems to have prevailed in Stiffkey.

Charlie Large, a retired wheelwright, has like Dick Dowsin, lived in the same village all his life. Charlie is the village poet and when he first heard of plans to shut down the Sun, he dashed off a few verses and ceremonially pinned his 'Curse on the brewers' to the door of the pub:

> 'Bad luck to all the brewers
> Who close up their pubs,
> May their profits dwindle
> And their wives all cease to love.

May they sit around the boardroom
With their faces drawn and glum,
May they forever rue the day
When they closed Old Buckenham Sun.

'This pub has been the same
For a hundred years or more,
With a good coal fire to heat it,
And pamments on the floor,
If you want a posh place
With carpets on the floor
Yes, you can have it
But the beer will cost you more.
So drink some home-made cider
And you will not give a damn
If they close all the bloody pubs
That belong to Watney Mann.'

Charlie has followed his own advice. He recovered a
butt from behind the Sun, and makes his own cider two
or three times a year from the apples that grow behind his
cottage. But it isn't true that he doesn't give a damn.
Charlie can't remember an evening from when he returned
from the First World War until the Sun was closed when
he didn't pop in for a couple of pints. He misses the
company so much that every so often he calls on Ernie and
Eileen Woodrow who used to run the pub and who bought
it to live in when it was closed. Eileen still keeps a few
bottles on the shelf for her old regulars when they call,
just to make it feel like 'home'. She misses the company
too, so much so that she helps out at the George in the
neighbouring village of New Buckenham.

Ernie and Eileen would have liked to keep the Sun as a
pub, even after Watneys had decided to sell it. But
Watneys were asking an additional £1,300 if the licence
was going to continue, together with a ten-year tie on beer,
spirits and cigarette supplies. The extra money was
beyond the means of the couple at the time, and in any

138

case they would have preferred to sell better beers than those that Watneys produce.

But why was it necessary to close the Sun, a popular pub that was often so full that customers spilled over into the kitchen and outside the back door? The answer lies in the second verse of Charlie Large's poem. It was a plain and simple pub that hadn't been modernised, which is probably one of the reasons why it was so popular. Watneys do not like such houses, and if they can't tart them up, prefer to shut them down instead of leaving them as they are, which is very often precisely the way the customers like them. Laurie Canham, Watneys regional trade director, says of the Sun that 'The premises were confined and of clay lump construction. We came to the conclusion that the capital cost of improving the Sun could never be commensurate with the trade that could be expected.'

The only brew that is available on Cake Street now, apart from the bottles that Eileen Woodrow keeps, is Charlie Large's home-made cider. The story is repeated throughout the county and Watneys in Norfolk have set a trend that is already spreading to other companies and to other rural areas. It is a dangerous trend, and even Watneys are to some extent aware of the damage they are doing. Their policy statement issued in 1969, that presaged the worst spate of closures, reads:

'Where it is felt that too many houses are located in any area for the available trade, only those are kept open which, either as they are or with improvements, will give the facilities needed. This applies even in marginal cases and when closure would produce hardship for the local population.'

In spite of the evidence to the contrary, and in spite of this admission, it was still possible for a Mr R. B. Sawrey-Cookson, who described himself as a Group Public Affairs Executive, to say to me from the company's London head office,

'We believe we have a good social conscience and that such decisions are arrived at fairly.' It is, of course, easy to say things like that when your own choice of the twelve nearest pubs involves no more journeying than five minutes on foot, or two in a taxi.

In country villages, the pub so often doubles up as a corner shop, bus shelter, or cricket pavilion. The effect of a pub closure on a local community can be just as disastrous in its own way as the withdrawal of the bus service. The difference between a village with a pub and one without is well illustrated in two of this chapter's photographs. While the people of Stoke Row in Oxfordshire gather happily outside their local, the villagers of Stiffkey have no glasses in their hands, but are reminded of what things used to be like by the former Townshend Arms behind them, and the water colours which were painted when it was still a pub. Thankfully there are a number of smaller brewers who realise the importance of the pub in village life. In East Anglia, the worst victim to date of pub closures, we have already discovered how Adnams of Southwold are extremely reluctant to close down pubs because their managing director cannot bear his company to be the instrument of killing off village life. Greene King, of Bury St Edmunds, have consistently re-affirmed their recognition of the community role the village pub plays, and have promised to sustain their contribution to this role. Charles Wells, of Bedford, recently demonstrated their commitment to the village pub when the Crown at Little Straughton, near St Neots, was burnt out early in 1972. Within two months of the fire, a temporary pub was deposited by crane next to the shell of the Crown, for use until the pub could be properly re-built. There are still parts of the country where the asset strippers have not been set loose on village life. It is to be hoped that they stay that way.

9. Pubs and the politicians

'What a glorious thing it will be if the Government brings our drinking laws into line with those of most European countries. Licensing laws will be abolished and with them the institution of the British pub.'

AUBERON WAUGH

Many people are suspicious of the intervention in industry of the Monopolies Commission and other official bodies. Dealing with such reviews of the brewing industry, Sir Alan Herbert once wrote:

'The politicians and social reformers have no canon laws to excuse their shunning; either they are ashamed to visit the ancient institution with which they perpetually meddle, or intellectual arrogance keeps them out. So they are ignorant, and if forty Licensing Commissions were to sit for forty years they would be as ignorant as before, because they will not consider the tavern inside the tavern with their fellow-men, but stand outside or sit in Whitehall, muttering inhuman phrases about 'redundancy' and 'licensed premises', and think they know their subject when they have got by heart the annual statistics of cirrhosis of the liver.'

Almost forty years to the month after those words were written, the Monopolies Commission published its 'Report on the Supply of Beer' in 1969. Among the findings of this report was that one of the consequences of the tied house system is that 'the elimination of inefficient, high-cost and redundant brewing capacity is retarded'. Or in other words, the sooner all the small breweries are shut down the better.

The Monopolies Commission Report was generally suspect in the way that Sir Alan Herbert had predicted.

143

It was suspect in other ways too, particularly in its reliance on information provided by the Brewers' Society and individual firms within the industry. 'It is exceptional,' wrote the Commissioners, 'for a public house not to have a public bar'. They concluded that the public bar did not require any statutory protection. Instead of eliciting worthless assurances, the Commissioners might have spent their time better by identifying trends objectively as the basis for their recommendations. Their failure to do so has left the public bar unprotected, and it is no longer exceptional to find a pub without a public bar. Already it is the rule in certain areas, and the trend is spreading. The Commissioners were also advised of the threat the tenants faced of being replaced by managers. They were given the following assurance:

'The (Brewers') Society states that ... no brewer is likely to terminate the tenancy of a tenant who is maintaining or increasing the value of trade in a pub.'

In the four years since the publication of the Commissioners report, hundreds of tenants have been given the boot in precisely the circumstances where the Brewers' Society claimed it was not 'likely' to happen.

The principal concern of the Monopolies Commission Report was to consider the future of the tied-house system—the system whereby the manufacturers own most of the outlets through which their products are retailed. It was found that, while the tie had always existed for beer supplies, it had been extended since the war to cover wines, spirits and cider by the vast majority of brewers, and at least half the brewers had tied their tenants for soft drink supplies, and over a quarter for cigarettes too. One instance of the brewers' increasing control over all the products sold in their pubs is particularly revealing. Not only do many tenants have to buy their whisky, for example, from their brewers, but it also has to be the brewers' own brand. Six ways in which such policies are implemented were described to the Commissioners by witnesses from the licensed trade. Firstly, as a tenant, if you order a different whisky from the one prescribed, you may find that a substitution has been made when you receive your supplies. Secondly, you may be able to order the brewers' own brand by the bottle, but all other brands only by the case. Thirdly, your order form might not include the alternatives you wish to purchase. Fourthly, you may be told that you can only place the brewers' own brand on optics. If you still persist in ordering what your customers really want, you may find, fifthly, that your deliveries arrive late, or sixthly, that your brewer will prove less than willing to spend money on the upkeep of your pub.

It is not surprising in the light of this kind of practice that the Commissioners concluded that the tied-house system operated against the public interest by enabling the brewers to restrict the choice of goods available to customers. Nevertheless, they did not recommend the abolition of the tied-house system, on the grounds that such a measure could do more damage than the system itself. They were probably right in this respect. If the small brewers lost their tied houses they would certainly find it harder to compete against the heavily promoted brands of the 'big six'. They would probably go out of business even faster than during the period in which the Commissioners were carrying out their investigations, when twenty brewers were taken over. It is unlikely, too, that the thousands of pubs which would come on the market as the result of such a measure would be purchased by the licensees who run them, and operated as free houses. They would probably be bought up in lots by property developers, or catering chains, who could be expected to do an even more severe asset-stripping job than the brewers themselves. These damaging effects of the abolition of the tied-house system still need to be borne in mind, in spite of the fact that the Monopolies Commission Report recommended that such a measure should not be taken. Early in 1973, more than 160 Labour MPs re-opened the issue by signing a motion calling for the breaking of the tie. This level of support indicates that the abolition of the tied-house system remains as a political possibility.

Even if the Commissioners were right to find that, although the tied-house system operates against the public interest, it should not be abolished, their conclusion does not help to solve a number of remaining problems. On the question of local monopolies for example, they also concluded that:

'Under the present tied house system there is, however, abnormally high concentration of ownership of public houses in certain areas. If there should be further mergers of large brewers, similar situations could occur in other areas.'

And of course, that is exactly what has happened, and continues to happen, further restricting the public's choice. It is current practice not to refer a particular bid or merger to the Monopolies Commission unless the enlarged company that results will control more than one third of the beer market. This is clearly not strict enough, as the ninety-odd companies within the industry could be reduced to less than half-a-dozen without any intervention from the Monopolies Commission. It is true that the government intends to introduce legislation in the 1973–74 parliamentary session under the Fair Trading Bill which will reduce the 'monopoly test' to 25 per cent of the market. Even if this is a step in the right direction, and possibly sufficient to cope with the problems of a number of industries, it will still leave the way open for many more damaging takeovers and mergers in the brewing industry. It would be more helpful to place the burden of proof that a particular takeover will benefit the public on

146

the bidding company, and to prevent such a takeover without the necessary proof.

A change of this kind could go a long way to protect the independent brewers and the public's choice, but it would not deal with the local monopolies that already exist. At a meeting of their Party Council in April 1973, the Liberals passed an interesting motion on the supply of beer, one clause of which deals with this problem. The motion in full called for:

(a) the original gravity of beers to be clearly marked;
(b) an end to brewery policy of replacing tenants with managers;
(c) an end to the restriction on what additional draught and bottled beers can be sold in tied houses;
(d) protests against the current brewery policies of replacing naturally conditioned beer with keg 'beers',;
(e) strong protests against the replacing of hand pumps with top pressure equipment;
(f) a full Monopolies Commission enquiry into the brewing trade, with a view to recommending the break-up of the present large combines.

There are a number of good points here, but the final clause, which espouses an approach already used in the United States to deal with harmful monopolies, is particularly relevant to the matter in question. Because this idea has its origins within a small party it is unlikely to be implemented in time to save the day, but it is a good idea and one that the major parties could study and perhaps adopt to the benefit of everyone concerned, excepting of course the 'big six' brewers.

As a result of their lengthy deliberations, the Monopolies Commission ended their report with a recommendation of sorts. This was that yet another study group should be set up to investigate the possibility of alleviating the worst effects of the tied-house system through a relaxation of the Licensing Laws. The Labour Govern-

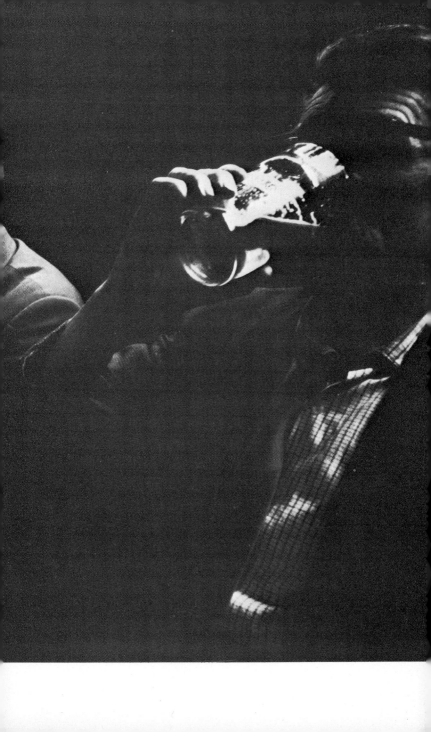

ment, nearing the end of its term of office, shelved even this timid recommendation. Their Conservative successors, however, appointed the Erroll Committee in 1970 to consider this recommendation, and the findings of the new committee were duly published in December, 1972.

The two principal recommendations of the Erroll Committee were as follows: firstly the abolition of the absolute discretion of local licensing justices to award or refuse a licence. This would be replaced by two statutory requirements, which, if a prospective licensee could satisfy them, would lead to the automatic award of a licence. These were that the licensee should be a fit person to operate his licence, and that his premises should be suitable from the point of view of structure, safety, and amenity. The second recommendation was that, with limited exceptions, pubs should be permitted to open at any time, and for any length of time, between ten in the morning and midnight. Times of opening and closing within these limits would be entirely at the licensee's discretion. In spite of the publicity given to the subject of 'children in pubs' at the time the Erroll Committee's findings were published, their consideration of this subject did not lead to any proposals that would have a significant impact on the nature of pubs—they merely suggested that a separate room on the premises could be provided for children at the licensee's discretion.

The two major recommendations would cause great changes if they were implemented. It is hard to fault the proposal that the basis of awarding a licence should be shifted from the licensing justices' interpretation of local 'need' to the suitability of the licensee and his premises. This would undoubtedly lead to a loosening of the tied-house system, and to a greater variety of places where one could go for a drink. Cafés with a more continental atmosphere would be given a chance to compete for custom with traditional pubs. It is only fair that they

150

should have this chance and that people should have the chance to use them.

The second recommendation bears on this question of atmosphere. Pubs would be able, if they wanted to, to open continuously for fourteen hours a day. The loss of the afternoon break could change the nature of those pubs whose atmosphere, particularly in the evening, depends on their filling up in the last hour before closing, rather than on people coming and going all the while during the day. Another point in favour of the afternoon break was made in a slightly intolerant but nevertheless relevant way, by Basil Boothroyd:

'You may be able to get a drink whenever you fancy one in those stained old crummy round-the-clock Continental bistros; only here in the land of the unfree, can we savour the springlike sensation, twice a day, of life beginning anew.'

There is a greater danger too, in these freer hours. It is that licensees will be pressed by their breweries to open longer than they do at the moment, and longer than they can reasonably be expected to if they are to have some free time of their own, instead of devoting themselves entirely to supplying the needs of other peoples' leisure. The Erroll Committee recognised this danger, and stressed that licensees must be protected against such pressure. But the brewers have many ways open to them to force their licensees into line (witness the evidence given to the Monopolies Commission on the question of the brewers' own brands of spirits). It is difficult to see how such protection could be effective against the underhand methods that would undoubtedly be adopted by the brewers in a number of cases.

The question of the Erroll Committee's recommendations is, for the moment, academic, as the Conservative government has shelved this report, just as the Labour government shelved that of the Monopolies Commission.

This is unfortunate as our Licensing Laws certainly need to be revised even if they do not need to be changed radically. It would have been possible to introduce the changes recommended by the Erroll Committee on an experimental basis in a limited area, until the government 'hived off' the State Management Scheme in Carlisle. The Carlisle Brewery, and the 130 pubs it supplied, had been run by the Home Office since the First World War until early in 1973, when the sale of these assets was completed. The brewery and the pubs were originally nationalised so that the drinking habits of local munitions workers could be controlled. Lloyd George announced at the time that:

'We are fighting Germany, Austria and drink, and the greatest of those deadly foes is drink.'

Obviously, the original need for nationalisation no longer applied, but there were many distressing features in the sale of the State Management Scheme. The brewery, extensively modernised in the 1960s, and well-known for the quality of its beer, has been closed. The beer now comes from Scotland, Tyneside, and Lancashire, from the breweries which have bought up the pubs. Ron Lewis, Carlisle's MP, was outraged by the sale and its likely effects on his constituents:

'The brewery produced excellent beers, suited to the local palate, and they were as cheap as any in the country. People in this area had come to appreciate the benefits of the scheme and they certainly didn't want it to be sold off. It was a modern, efficient, and consistently profitable concern, so the taxpayers won't benefit from the sale either. The darts leagues and the whist leagues and so on are unlikely to survive the sale, and I can just see the new owners ripping up the bowling greens to put car parks there instead. There was no justification for this sale and it will do a lot of damage to the local community.'

Ron Lewis seems to be right. There was no justification

for the sale of the State Management Scheme, at least in the way it was handled. Immediately prior to the 1970 general election, Quintin Hogg, Shadow Home Secretary at the time, said:

'It is increasingly obvious that it is thoroughly inappropriate for the Home Office to be directly concerned in a commercial operation of this kind. We shall therfore be ready to consider any viable proposal for transferring the ownership and management of the State Scheme to a suitably constituted local body, such as a trust.'

This would have been a sensible re-organisation, with the honourable precedent of the Carlsberg Foundation in Denmark, whose profits are spent on the arts and the sciences in that country. It is clear that the government had no mandate to break the business up and close the brewery down in the way that they did. Their actions were even condemned by the northern branch of the Monday Club, usually an out-and-out supporter of total free enterprise. And now, in one more region of the country, customers have to pay more for products they like less.

It is hard to escape the conclusion that our politicians prefer either to do nothing at all or, when they do stir themselves, to do positive harm to the interests of the people who use pubs in this country. This is tragic at a time when so much needs to be done if those pubs that have not already been damaged by the brewers are to be preserved. The worst effects of the tied-house system clearly need to be controlled. Takeovers and mergers within the brewing industry, which will further restrict the public's range of choice, need to be prevented. Tenant licensees need to be protected against eviction. People who drink beer should be informed of the strength of what they are buying, not so that they can always go for the strongest, but so that they will know when their brew is being watered down, and by how much. The term

'draught', in relation to beer, needs to be registered with a definition under the Trade Descriptions Act so that it cannot be used to describe fizzy keg and top pressure beers. The use of increasing amounts of extracts and chemical substitutes in the brewing process ought to be stopped. Local monopolies need to be challenged and broken up. The Licensing Justices must be directed to look much more critically at schemes for tarting up pubs and removing their public bars. The failure of successive governments to take action on these lines has enabled the brewers to go their own way without regard for the public interest. Unless action is taken soon, the future in our pubs will be even more bleak, and more universally bleak, than the present already is.

10. Through a glass darkly

'It may be that you will be able to travel round cities in a Hover Bar in which one can have a drink while travelling from point to point. Managers will more than likely be running automated pubs with no barmaids.'

KENNETH SAXBY, Director, Scottish and Newcastle Breweries.

If at first you think that's a joke, think again. Scottish and Newcastle are already getting into practice to translate this vision into reality. The *Brewers' Guardian* wrote of their 'Silver Wing' in Edinburgh:

'The Concorde Room is dominated by a colour photomural of the aircraft taking off, and part of the room is equipped with mock aircraft seating, lights, luggage rack, pressure windows, etc. The main section is designed like an airport waiting lounge. The noise of passing aircraft to and from Turnhouse Airport adds realism to the theme.'

Hover Bars, Concorde Rooms, why not a Lunar Lounge? You can just imagine the press handout:

'Imperial United Cement (Holdings) Limited, who were pleased to welcome the brewing operations of British Insulated Fibres into their chemical engineering division after the merger of the two companies earlier this year, are equally delighted to announce the opening of the new group's first brand new pub. The main feature of The Space Age, which replaces the demolished Pig and Whistle on the same site, is its Crater Bar, the brainchild of leading London pub designer Simon Hiley-Smoothe, who fashioned it with the assistance of the plastics sub-division of our tied estate building department.

The automated bar has a mission control push-button fascia, based on designs obtained from Houston. The landlord's traditional cry of "Time Gentlemen, Please" will be replaced

157

by a tape-recording of the countdown for the recent moonshot Apollo Thirty-Six. Blast-off comes at 10.40 p.m. during the week and at 11.10 p.m. on Fridays and Saturdays.

Customers suffering from weightlessness as a result of the heavily carbonated range of beers on sale at The Space Age, may leave their cars overnight in the Module Park, and be driven home in the pub's own moon buggy.'

The pubs of the future *will* include automated service. The idea is not just a brewer's dream or an author's nightmare. Watneys have already experimented with beer dispense machines at The Stag near London's Victoria Station.

It seems likely, too, that the beers of tomorrow will be even worse than the worst of today's. Tanks will replace casks and even kegs until each pub cellar is a massive storage container. Drays that look more like petrol tankers will call round once a fortnight to top them up. Professor Hough of the British School of Malting at Birmingham University predicted in 1972 that we would soon be drinking raspberry, strawberry and other fruit-flavoured beers. On cue as always, one of the big six was already test-marketing an orange beer, and this is now generally available. A pint of orange today, a pint of strawberry tomorrow. The market research teams might even get round to the idea of vanilla flavoured beer if they reverse the spectrum of their thinking as applied to ice cream. Come back, Wicked Lady, all is forgiven!

It isn't at all alarmist to suggest that a pint of bitter may soon be a thing of the past. Our recent entry into the Common Market has posed a new threat to the hop farms of Kent. The distinctive flavour of English beer is only made possible by the fact that we have always allowed male hops to grow alongside the female plants, and fertilisation to take place. European hops are exclusively female, chaste, and seedless. They make good lager, but they don't make English beer. If our hop growers decide to compete in Europe now that the tariff barriers are down,

158

they will have to tear up the male plants from their fields. If they decide to do this, they will achieve overnight what the big six haven't quite achieved in ten year's effort, the universal death of traditional English beer.

Whether this happens or not, new-style beer will be served in the new-style pubs. The brewers would have us believe that the voices raised in opposition to these changes speak in tones of sheer sentimentality. It may be that beer which has no taste (unless fruit-flavoured), and pubs that are designed in appalling taste, will find a number of adherents. But there are millions of people who have money in their pockets that they would prefer to spend on a variety of traditional products in a variety of traditional atmospheres, if what remains of this choice is allowed to survive.

Flavour and variety have not only died in the English pub. The flavour has gone from many foods, from bread to frozen vegetables, on through sweating cheeses to sawdust sausages. The word 'variety' that used to have a special meaning in the world of entertainment, doesn't carry that meaning any more. Our cinemas and our theatres rest in even fewer hands than our pubs; often, their output is even more geared to the space age than that of our breweries. Indeed, it is one of the favourite arguments of the brewers, and their representative body, The Brewers' Society, to point out that 'we're part of the leisure industry now, and we've got to compete,' a claim that is partly true, but mainly misleading.

There are many ways in which, as the pub develops, it is bound to reflect, and needs to reflect, other sectors of society. But there is also a sense in which it should not be a sheer blinded reflector of the bright lights elsewhere. The pub is a refuge from, as well as part of, society. It is a place that we use to relax from the pressures elsewhere. When we can no longer lean on our local in this way, modern society will have blown another safety valve.

And even if the brewers have been slower and more reluctant to kill off flavour and variety than the sausage makers or the cinema owners, that is all the more reason why we should be concerned with their activities. This is one corpse that can still be revived.

There must surely come a point at which unwilling consumers will resist unwelcome change. The big six have set up their signposts for the future. At the same time they have tried to block off the by-roads at the end of which pubs still feel like pubs, and beer still tastes like beer. Perhaps it is up to the people who care about these things, and the politicians who represent them, to open up those by-roads and to pull those signposts down.